What Gave Giving A Bad Name

Sermons on Stewardship

David A. Shirey

CSS Pubishing Company
Lima, Ohio

WHAT GAVE GIVING A BAD NAME?

Library of Congress Cataloging-in-Publication Data

Names: Shirey, David A., 1959- author.
Title: What gave giving a bad name? : stewardship sermons that stir generosity / David Shirey.
Description: Lima, Ohio : CSS Publishing Company, [2024] | Includes bibliographical references.
Identifiers: LCCN 2024021059 (print) | LCCN 2024021060 (ebook) | ISBN 9780788031151 (paperback) | ISBN 9780788031168 (adobe pdf)
Subjects: LCSH: Christian giving. | Christian stewardship.
Classification: LCC BV772 .S523 2024 (print) | LCC BV772 (ebook) | DDC 248/.6--dc23/eng/20240605
LC record available at https://lccn.loc.gov/2024021059
LC ebook record available at https://lccn.loc.gov/2024021060

For more information about CSS Publishing Company resources, visit our website at www.csspub.com, email us at csr@csspub.com, or call (800) 241-4056.

e-book:
ISBN-13: 978-0-7880-3116-8
ISBN-10: 0-7880-3116-3

ISBN-13: 978-0-7880-3115-1
ISBN-10: 0-7880-3115-5

"Who then is that faithful and wise steward?" (Luke 2:42, KJV)To be faithful stewards of the eight congregations I served over four decades of ministry and to Jennie who, every Sunday morning for forty years, has written the check for our offering at the breakfast table.

Contents

Preface

A poll was taken among preachers. The question was, "What is your least favorite part of ministry?" The top response was the annual stewardship campaign. And I can't help but believe that if a similar poll were taken among churchgoers, the response would be the same. Like preacher, like congregation.

Christian stewardship is not my least favorite part of ministry. Far from it. I actually enjoy the challenge of crafting sermons that invite joyful generosity.

What gave giving a bad name, anyway? How did give become a four-letter word?

A decade ago, Dean Snyder, senior pastor of Foundry United Methodist Church in Washington, DC, wrote about how some pastors, in order to avoid saying the word money in church, resort to all kinds of verbal gymnastics that invite giving everything but money[1] — such as, "our time and talent," "our hearts, minds, and souls," "our best thoughts by day and by night," etc. As if money and its proper and improper use is of no concern to God. It is. As if scripture says nothing about giving money. It does. As if the church could do just fine if everybody gave generously of their time and talent but nothing of their treasure. It wouldn't.

I know some folks have been in churches where they have been badgered, cajoled, guilt-tripped, and arm-twisted into giving. That's distasteful to be sure. But I for one have found that in structuring my budget around God's invitation to give my first 10% through the church, save 10%, and live on the rest, my wife and I have managed to make it through forty years pretty well. So I have no problem inviting my brothers and sisters in Christ to return thanks by giving generously so as to partner with God and our risen Lord in redeeming and blessing all creation.

Twenty-five years ago or so, Psychology Today published a piece about the correlation between giving and "ethical living."[2]

The magazine did a reader survey on ethics and morals, seeking to determine what factors influence morality. For example, if the reader slightly scratched someone's car and no one saw, would the reader drive away? Would the reader ever take sick leave when they weren't sick? Would they take liberties on their tax return? Would they tell a lie?

Some 24,000 people returned the questionnaire. Seventy-one percent claimed to be at least slightly religious while twenty-nine percent claimed to be not religious at all. Was one group more moral than others? Older respondents seemed to be more ethical than younger ones, but only slightly. Income level made no difference, nor did education, marital status, or occupation.

The factor the survey found to be the most accurate predictor of a person having a moral/ethical compass was whether they were generous or not. Apparently, the more tightly people hold to their money, the less willing they are to give generously to others, and the less likely they are to make decent and honorable decisions in the scores of ethical dilemmas in which they find themselves daily. Somebody told me to be wary of two kinds of people: those who do not like animals and those who do not have a sense of humor. I'm adding a third category: those who lack generosity. There's good reason the word miser is at the root of the word miserable.

By contrast, generosity born of gratitude is good for us. Researchers did a study with several hundred people measuring how gratitude contributes to well-being. One group was asked to keep a journal noting all the events that happened in their day. A second group was instructed to note only the unpleasant things. A third group was told to list the things that happened each day for which they were grateful. After three weeks, those in the group who kept gratitude lists showed "higher levels of alertness, enthusiasm, determination, and less stress. They also felt more loved and were more inclined toward acts of kindness."[3] Which goes to show that an attitude of gratitude that manifests itself in generosity is good for the soul, while clutching, grasping, and hoarding is not good for anybody.

Christians don't need "Psychology Today" and a cadre of researchers to tell us that. The Bible tells us so. Giving is a good thing — for my own good, for the good of others, and for the healing of all creation.

Here are a collection of sermons culled from forty years of preaching and teaching financial stewardship that strive to give giving a good name. Knowing full well how my preaching on giving has been inspired by others' stewardship sermons, I hope these sermons will pay forward a debt of gratitude. Even more, I hope they bear faithful witness to the men and women, pastors and lay members, who lived lives seasoned with joyful generosity. The spirit in which they lived their lives, much more than the words they preached, taught, or spoke, kindled within me the desire to be a good and faithful steward. I am merely passing on to you what I first received.

A word about how these sermons are ordered follows this preface. Allow me to provide a few introductory remarks about them.

All were preached as part of annual stewardship campaigns inviting pledges of financial support for the coming year's ministry and mission. The language associated with such efforts varies from church to church (pledges, estimates of giving, commitment cards, annual fund, stewardship emphasis). Adapt the language to your setting.

Likewise, though I made the transition from the language and practices of in person worship (offering plates, pledge cards, and snail mail) to the post-COVID language and practices of hybrid in person and online worship (web sites, giving portals, QR codes, and direct deposit), the sermons are not uniform in their vocabulary for the means of giving. Adapt the language to your emerging practices.

The language in these sermons is conversational in style. Preaching is an aural enterprise; to be heard, not read. As such, my personal practice has always been to write for my voice. So don't take a red pen to my grammar or incomplete sentences. These sermons were written to be spoken aloud with accompanying facial and hand gestures, pauses, emphasis on certain words and phrases, the occasional singing of verses of hymns and popular music (likely off key), and numerous smirks, chuckles, and rolls of the eyes. Translate my language into your voice and make the message come alive in your own inimitable way.

Emily Dickinson said, "Tell the truth but tell it slant," brilliant advice that counsels communicating important truths in creative, indirect ways. Jesus' parables are a case in point. The Master comes alongside his hearers and tells what at first blush is a simple story but at tale's end, a door opens wide and a plethora of meaning beckons the listener's attention. Preaching on financial stewardship calls for the same strategy. So, though there is plenty of straightforward rhetoric in these sermons, there are many examples of telling the truth "slant" — segments preached with tongue firmly in cheek or facetiously, with feigned disbelief or downright silliness. I'll stoop or rise to any level, whatever it takes to tell the truth slant, the truth that we have been blessed beyond measure by a gracious God who welcomes our partnership heart, mind, soul, and wallet.

Last and not least, it is my firm belief that sermonic content born of exegetical and theological acumen and rhetorical craftsmanship, creativity, and cleverness must be accompanied by preachers' and church leaders' personal practice of faithful stewardship. We can't ask others to do what we don't do ourselves. I intentionally bear witness in these sermons to my own journey toward being a good and faithful steward. I wasn't always a good steward and I duly acknowledge that. But thanks to the example, teaching, and inspiration of others, many of whom are acknowledged in these pages, I have grown and matured across the years to where I can honestly, sincerely, even gleefully bear witness to the quiet joy and deep down satisfaction that accrues with giving of myself more and more fully to God's purposes. Bear witness in your own words to your growth in and practice of financial stewardship.

Grace and peace to you in your preaching, teaching, and being a good steward of God's manifold graces.

A Word About The Order Of The Sermons

The first four sermons ("What Gave Giving A Bad Name?" "Things My Father Never Taught Me," "Giving By The Book," and "Pointers From Paul's Playbook") address the problem and offer encouragement to proceed with gospel-grounded courage. The problem is congregations chafing against hearing sermons on financial stewardship (They're always talking about money!") and preachers fretting over preaching them ("Do I have to preach about money again?"). The encouragement comes from sermons crafted to penetrate those defenses by a strategy that leavens solid biblical teaching dished out in fresh ways with self-deprecating humor and enthusiasm.

The next three sermons ("A Most Delicate Issue," "The Macedonian Miracle," and "Something Beautiful For God") mine three iconic stewardship scriptures for their riches. The stories of the widow's mite, the unnamed woman's anointing of Jesus' feet, and the Macedonian Christians' offering to the first stewardship campaign are motivational gems, examples of joyful generosity par excellence. These stories and the sermons they give voice to make giving gladly invitational, even aspirational: I want to give like that when I grow up!

There is no getting around the fact that annual stewardship campaigns include an ask. We're blessed to be a blessing, invited as people of faith to give of our time, talent, and treasure to God's redeeming purposes in this world. We have a choice whether to give, to whom, and how much. The next two sermons ("Holy Choices" and "Where Treasure, There Heart") explore the consequences of our decisions. They are followed by two sermons ("Pass The Plates" and "All God's Chil'ren Got Talent") that surface surprising new insights into two specific asks: our tithe and our talent.

The penultimate sermons ("A Great Commandment Congregation" and "The Master's Math") link giving to partnering with God in the redeeming of all creation. Spare us from stewardship sermons that try to motivate giving by drear obligation clothed in shoulds and oughts. Though there may have been a time when people responded to stewardship campaigns out of a sense of duty and commitment, that time and those generations are no more. Rising generations must be confident that the people inviting their gifts are authentic, sincere, and trustworthy and the organizations and institutions they give to are making a transforming difference in the world. People give to people. Money follows mission.

The final sermon ("The Indescribable Gift") grounds stewardship in God's "indescribable gift" of Jesus Christ. The gospel he came preaching, teaching, and living was, by definition, good news. So must our preaching about stewardship be good news. May your proclamation give giving a good name. If these sermons in any way contribute to that end by glorifying God and serving others in the name of Jesus Christ, that will be good news to me.

What Gave Giving A Bad Name?

2 Corinthians 8:1-7

A poll was taken among preachers. The question was, "What is your least favorite part of the ministry?" What do you think the top response was? The most-mentioned least favorite was the annual stewardship campaign. I can't help but believe that if a similar poll were to be taken among the laity, the response would be the same. I suspect that one of the least-anticipated events on the church calendar is the annual stewardship campaign. Like preacher, like congregation. Think of that: inviting people to give to the cause of Jesus Christ by pledging a portion of their money to his church is one of the least favorite things that preachers and members of their congregations do in a year. All of which raises this simple question, "What gave giving a bad name?"

Well, I've given that question some thought and I'm prepared to put forth what I think gave giving such a bad name.

For starters, it strikes me that giving doesn't come naturally to us. There is something deep down inside us that makes us against giving from the start. I say that because I can't help but to notice that when I put my finger in an infant's open palm, he or she will grasp it and hold on to it and will not let go, as if maybe we're born with the inclination to grasp and hold on to things. And I can't help but notice that as kids acquire speech they become quite adept at calling out the names of the holy trinity at the top of their lungs. Not Father, Son, and Holy Spirit, mind you, but rather "Me! My! Mine!" as if they're born with those words in their vocabulary. I can't help but to remember the exchange that my wife and I engaged in prior to our move from St. Louis years ago, the exact same exchange we had a few years before that when moving from Nashville.

Looking out over our belongings, I said, "Where on earth did we get all this stuff?"

She replied, "Well, what do you want to get rid of?"

I replied, "Well, some of your stuff. I need all my stuff."

In that moment, I felt like an old magnet I found one day in a desk drawer, coated with paper clips, pins, and every metal do-dad imaginable. Is there something within me that attracts, accumulates, and holds on to, but never lets go of, anything that comes within my sphere of influence? It seems as if grasping, "me! my! mine-ing!", hoarding, and never letting go are what come naturally to human beings. It's giving, sharing, and letting go that go against the grain. That would explain why the annual stewardship campaign is a perennial least-favorite thing, why it's greeted with such groans ("Here they go again!"), why it's tolerated with such grudging spirits, and why pen is put to pledge card with such painful reluctance. It seems giving is contrary to human nature. It rubs us the wrong way. Maybe it's human nature that gave giving a bad name.

But there's more to it than that. There's also the notion, deep-seated in all of us, that we don't have a whole lot to give. We've convinced ourselves that we really don't have much. How can we give when we're barely getting by on what we have? This brings to mind a poll that was done a few years back. The question was asked, "How much more would you need to make in order to be more secure?" The answer was, "About 20% more than I make now." Regardless of whether the person interviewed made $30,000 or $130,000, the answer was the same — I need 20 % more. This tells me that if we've convinced ourselves that we simply don't have anything to give (given the little we have), then no wonder the annual stewardship campaign is among our least-favorite things. It's asking us to do what we really can't do. How can we be expected to give away something when we don't have enough in the first place? So, maybe that's what gave giving a bad name.

On the other hand, maybe giving got its bad name from some of the abuses we've seen in past years. You know what

I mean — the TV evangelists and their incessant asks for donations. It has come to the point that when I stand up in the pulpit and mention money, you probably envision a toll-free number parading across the screen right under my chin. You hear me mention giving and you subconsciously push the mute button -"Oh boy, here he goes again. Where there's a preacher, there's an offering plate not far behind." Maybe that's why the stewardship campaign is listed as least favorite on so many ballots. "All they talk about is money and then look how they use what they get!" Maybe that's what gave giving a bad name.

Or maybe it's a combination of all of the above that gave giving a bad name. In the first place, it's against our nature to give, so it rubs us the wrong way when we're asked. What's more, we don't have enough as it is, and even if we did, "Who are you going to trust these days to give it to?"

Having said all that, what do you make of this? I know some folks who gave giving a good name. I have discovered in my research a pastor and a congregation for whom the annual stewardship campaign was not something to be dreaded and endured, but rather something to be done with a spirit of expectation and joy: "I want you to know, brothers and sisters, about the grace of God that has been granted to the churches of Macedonia, for during a severe ordeal of affliction their abundant joy and their extreme poverty have overflowed in a wealth of generosity on their part. For, as I can testify, they voluntarily gave according to their means and even beyond their means, begging us earnestly for the favor of [giving]" (2 Corinthians 8:1-14).

You heard me right: a congregation that actually begged for the favor of giving! I have it all right here in black and white in a letter from their preacher, a fellow by the name of Paul. What do you make of this? In all my years in the church, I've never seen anything like it before. Contrary to human nature, they begged for the favor of being invited to give. Contrary to the reluctance you and I are familiar with, their giving was accompanied by an abundance of joy — they were downright cheerful givers.

If that were not enough, these folks really didn't have enough. They were truly poor. But surprise, surprise — "out of their extreme poverty there overflowed a wealth of liberality." They gave according to their means and beyond. Beats anything I've ever seen. These folks gave giving a good name.

Which got me to wondering. I asked myself, "How did they do it?" I mean, with all there is to give giving a bad name and with the way most churches and preachers enter into the annual stewardship campaign kicking and screaming, what did they do differently?

According to their preacher, Paul, there was a turning point all right. There was a point when, for those people and for that preacher, give ceased being a four-letter word and became something they took great pleasure in doing. What was the turning point? "First, they gave themselves to the Lord..." (2 Corinthians 8:5). They took Jesus Christ as their Lord and Savior and pledged to love the Lord their God with all their heart, soul, might, and mind. Having done that, all their treasure followed, and joyfully at that! Which is to say that when a congregation and pastor give themselves first to the Lord, it makes all the difference in the world. Hearts are warmed, attitudes are changed, and human nature is transformed. In other words, giving is given a good name. When people truly give themselves to the Lord, hands that before held, grasped, and hoarded, find themselves finally able to open up, let go, and give. Voices that before growled, "Mine!" find themselves finally able to say "Thine!" When people truly give themselves to the Lord first, hearts are filled to overflowing with the unspeakable riches of God's grace to the point that I know I am rich and so I want to give to the one from whom all blessings flow.

Do you know that it still happens today? When people give themselves first to the Lord, heart, might, mind, and soul, giving is given a good name. Extraordinary things happen. Spirits soar. Pledges are made with reverent pleasure.

Yes, it still happens today. I went to a church one day last year, went into worship, and wouldn't you know, I happened to be there on the very Sunday they were doing their stewardship campaign. I must admit, I rolled my eyes and said, "Oh boy." They had a preacher there who launched into some stewardship thing, and then they passed out pledge cards and I took one just because everybody else did and I sat there all uncomfortable. (You see, giving had been given such a bad name in my book.) But then something happened I'll never forget.

As I sat in this church, pledge card in hand — I'm speaking about our church — I lifted my eyes and saw you give what I could tell was prayerful attention to your cards. Then, as I watched, you stepped out of the pews, came down the aisle, and put your cards in the silver bowl in front of the communion table. As you did, I noticed a look of worshipful reverence in your eyes — you looked like I thought you must have looked when you first came down the aisle to make your confession of faith those many years ago. Then it dawned on me, that's exactly what you folks in this church were doing. Sure enough, you were giving yourselves first to the Lord, giving yourselves again, giving yourselves gladly, and your giving gladly followed. Then I watched as the people in this church made their way back to the fellowship hall for dinner. When the report was finally read and so many had given out of their own means and even beyond with an overflowing of liberality, one of our long-time members came up to me and with wide-eyed amazement said, "Well, that beats anything I've ever seen!" I didn't ask her to explain. I understood. She was experiencing the same thrill Paul had experienced. It is the thrill that comes when people give of themselves first to the Lord, the thrill that comes when Christians give giving a good name.

Let all God's people say AMEN.

Things My Father Never Taught Me

Deuteronomy 6:4-9

These verses are at the very heart of the Bible. They are often referred to as the Shema, from the Hebrew word for hear or listen that begins them: "Hear, O Israel: The Lord is our God, the Lord alone. You shall love the Lord your God with all your heart and with all your soul and with all your might." Deuteronomy says these words are so important they are to be taught to the children. "Recite them to your children and talk about them when you are at home and when you are away, when you lie down and when you rise."

You know something is important if an entire community is commanded to teach it to their children. The important things in life we teach our children. Or at least, we should. Beginning with how to use the potty. How to use a spoon. How to get dressed. How to write your name. The three Rs: Readin', Writin' and 'Rithmetic. Then came things like how to bathe yourself and how to make your bed. Things like how to swim and common courtesies: "Please" and "Thank you." Then came the advanced lessons: Skills, crafts, home repair, sports, and values. You know something is important if rising generations take the time and effort to teach it to their children.

That having been said, this week I've been pondering the things my father didn't teach me. Don't get me wrong; there were plenty of things Keith Shirey taught his eldest son. For instance, how to give a firm handshake. "Don't give someone a dead fish," he'd say. How to tie a necktie — a double Windsor knot and how to polish shoes and wax a car (How many times did I wax his car?). Among other things, he also taught me to treat everyone, no matter their station in life, with respect, to always do my best, to persevere through adversity, and to root for the Cleveland Browns (an exercise in persevering through adversity). Those are things he taught me.

There were things, however, about which my dad never taught me. To name three: religion, sex, and money. I dare say those are important things, things about which a child ought be taught, but none of them were in my father's curriculum.

As for religion, Dad simply didn't give the things of God much thought during his lifetime, at least as far as I could tell. When I got interested in faith issues, he asked my mother to ask me not to talk about religion around him. He was uncomfortable with it. Just didn't want to talk about it. So, I didn't.

I guess he didn't want to talk with me about sex, either. When I was about ten years old or so, Dad and I were waiting in the car for my mother, sister, and brother. I was in the back seat minding my own business when Dad, without even turning around, said, "David, there are some books in my closet on the shelf above where I hang my ties. Read them and if you have any questions ask me."

"What kind of books?" I asked.

"Well, they're red books," he responded.

"What are they about?"

He said, "You'll see. Just read 'em."

End of conversation.

It wasn't until I went upstairs later that week, got the books down, and began leafing through them that I saw what they were about. But I'll be doggoned if I was going to ask Dad any questions about that. If he couldn't even look me in the eye and say the word, why would I think he'd openly discuss any of the intimate details?

Dad was closed-lipped on religion, sex, and on money, too. I can't recall a single conversation having anything to do with money: what he made, his plans for the use of it, or the strategies he employed to save or invest it. There was not a word on how to write a check, balance a budget, read a financial report or make a wise investment. Certainly nothing was said about giving money away — how much, to whom, and why.

That is all to say that I learned a lot from my father, but I wanted to do better than he did teaching my children about at least three things: religion, sex, and money.

That's why this morning and next week I'd like to do my part by providing accurate information on two important subjects. I'm not going to talk about sex today or next week (though I do have some red books you can borrow). I am going to talk about religion and money, though. Not just because we have an opportunity this month to think about those two things as they converge at the point of making an estimate of giving to God to support the ministries of our church, but because in the absence of my father's teaching me anything about the whys and wherefores of giving to God, I've had to disabuse myself of a whole lot of notions about the intersection of religion and money — giving — that are at best misleading and at worst simply false. I don't want my children or my church family to labor under some of the misinformation I've heard out there in the neighborhood.

In one of his sermons years ago, Dr. Ron Allen, professor emeritus of preaching at Christian Theological Seminary, named a few of these misguided myths[4]. I'll name them for you and add a few of my own.

For instance, I was led to believe for a while that giving to the church was something you had to do to earn God's favor. That if I gave, God would love me — and if I gave more, God would love me more. And if I didn't give, well we won't go there. I'm glad I've learned that is blatantly false.

God's love for us is unconditional. God's love for us doesn't rise or fall one iota based on how much we do or do not give. Fundamental to the Christian faith is that God loves us period. "He makes his sun rise on the evil and on the good and sends rain on the righteous and on the unrighteous" (Matthew 5:45). I'm glad I learned that God's love for me is unconditional and has nothing to do with what I do or do not give.

For a while, too, I was led to believe that the biblical practice of making a pledge — setting aside a certain percentage of my income as a weekly offering to God — was the religious equivalent of paying a bill. I learned that, I think, from a woman in my first church who would come by periodically, stick her head in my office, show me her offering envelope, and say, "I just came by to pay my dues." What? Like her membership would be cancelled if she didn't pay them?

> *Dear Mrs. So-and-so, our records show that your church payments are past due. Please send your check in the amount noted at the bottom of the pink invoice and return it to our billing office at your earliest convenience so that we won't have to cancel your subscription to "Salvation, Inc". Return your offering now and you won't miss a single exciting issue.*

I don't like paying bills or dues, so I was glad when I learned that the biblical tithe has nothing to do with paying dues and everything to do with giving gifts. Once I got past the dues paying and into the gift giving mentality, not only did I give more, but I did so with delight. My check wrapped in an offering envelope says From: David, Jennie, Will, Betsy, and Laura To: God. I love giving gifts to the one who has so richly gifted me.

Another thing I'm glad I unlearned is the notion that suggests tithing or giving is some kind of quid pro quo business transaction with God. Tithing as investment strategy. Do you know this one? Here's the deal: you give God 10% and God will give you a return on your investment like you wouldn't believe.

TV evangelists parlay this one to great effect complete with testimonies like, "I gave to God the little bit I had and that very week I received some cash in the mail that was ten times what I had given! And you, too, can be blessed if you call 1-800-SEND-CASH." That's a caricature, of course. But it's out there and with it, the motivation for giving becomes greed: giving so you'll get more back.

Thank God a man named Bill taught me the lie in that.

"David," said that lifelong tither and benefactor of so many worthy organizations, "the notion of 'Give and get rich off God' is nothing but sanctified selfishness."

He said, "I can testify to having been blessed as a result of my tithing. Setting aside the first 10% for God required me to budget the remaining 90% well and spend it wisely. This lifelong discipline I have no doubt has led to the financial health I enjoy today, but I didn't give to get back. I gave and have experienced how God gives back the inestimable satisfaction that comes with partnering with God in making a difference in people's lives near and far."

Bill didn't give in order to get. But in giving, he got. I'm glad he taught me that because Jennie and I can testify to the fact that in our years of tithing we have received kingdom dividends year in and year out that have outperformed every other investment we've ever made.

I'm glad, too, I was liberated from the notion I had picked up along the way from certain folks that money and religion — giving an offering to God — is somehow something dirty and therefore not to spoken of in mixed company. That's what it seemed like to me, anyway. I've witnessed the contortions Christian people go through to downplay the Bible's invitation to give generously to God's redeeming work in this world. As if the words freewill offering are some form of profanity. As if give is a four-letter word.

I remember as a young, wet-behind-the-ears pastor in my mid-twenties making a visit to new members of the church I served. A member of the congregation and I took to their home all kinds of things that would help them become acquainted with and involved in the life of our congregation. We handed out a pictorial directory, a constitution and by-laws (whoopee!), a Sunday school schedule, a budget, and explained the opportunities for worship, education, and service that were available for that new brother and sister's growth in faith.

At the end of the night, as we were standing on the doorstep saying good-bye, my partner reached into his pocket and slyly sat something down on a shelf to the side of the door.

He whispered to the new members, "I'll just set these down over here and if you want to use them, you can. If you have questions, call."

By the guarded tone of his voice, I wondered what kind of contraband he had brought with him. I expected to see my dad's red books! You know what it was? Offering envelopes.

I'm glad I've met people over the years of my life who talk openly, humbly, and joyfully about what they give to God and why and the satisfaction they've found in doing so. Far from sounding like they're ashamed or embarrassed, far from sounding like they're whispering some sordid stuff not fit for mixed company, their talking about giving is a reveling in the privilege and pleasure of returning thanks to God.

What I'm saying is that in the absence of my father's teaching me openly about such things as religion and money, I'm grateful for having unlearned some of the misinformation and falsehoods that are out there.

I'm glad I've learned to see giving to God in its proper, biblical light: as a gift given in gratitude for all God has given me, shared with my church family and with people near and far.

Where did I learn the right attitude toward giving? Well, from the Bible. And I learned through the cadre of faithful stewards I've met in congregations I've served. But most all through something that happened to me in June of 1984. That's when I married Jennie Taylor.

When we were engaged and were sharing our values, hopes, and dreams, she said, "It's important to me that we tithe — set aside at least the first 10% of our income to God, the greatest portion of that going to whatever church we belong to and the rest to organizations we feel make a difference for good in our world."

I said, "Tithe? 10%? That's not something my parents ever taught me."

I had just received my letter of call to my first church. It was May 1985. My salary and housing allowance added up to

$19,000. I did the math—a tithe would be $1,900. Divided by 52 equaled $36.52 a week. My Dad did teach me math. I thought to myself: $36.52 a week! Yikes! Everything in me constricted.

To which my fiancée said, "That's a tithe and it's important to me that we do that in our marriage. God is good. We'll have enough."

My father never taught me that.

The most important things in life we teach our children. "Recite them to your children and talk about them when you are at home and when you are away, when you lie down and when you rise." It was clear to me in my talking with Jennie those years ago that as a child she had learned truths about giving I hadn't learned at all.

I asked her, "Where did you get your perspective on giving?"

She said, "It's something my father taught me."

What he taught her, I'll teach you next week.

Giving By The Book

Matthew 24:45-47

Jesus asked great questions — loaded questions. For example:

- "What are you looking for?" (John 1:38)
- "What is it you want me to do for you?" (Mark 10:36)
- "Do you want to be made well?" (John 5:6)
- "Why do you call me 'Lord, Lord,' and not do what I tell you?" (Luke 6:46)

Every one of those questions is a great conversation starter as is the question Jesus asks in this morning's passage: "Who is the wise and faithful steward?" (Matthew 24:45). Some translations of the Bible (NRSV) have, "Who is the wise and faithful slave?" Others (NIV, KJV) have, "Who is the wise and faithful servant?" The Greek word doulos can be translated servant or slave. But this servant/slave's job description is to faithfully manage someone else's possessions. That's what a steward does. The dictionary defines a steward as "a person who manages the property, finances or other affairs for someone else." I'm going to translate Jesus' question as "Who is a wise and faithful steward?"

Biblically speaking, God has appointed us stewards of all there is. Psalm 24 says, "The earth is the Lord's and all that is in it" (Psalm 24:1). In other words, we're property managers. And everything is God's property. Which means all we have is not ours to do with as we please, but ours to use and manage in ways that please God. As a hymn sings it,

"We give Thee but thine own, whate'er the gift may be; all that we have is thine alone, a trust, O Lord, from thee."5

That brings us back to Jesus' question: "Who then is the wise and faithful steward?" Or to personalize Jesus' question, "Am

I a wise and faithful steward?" That begs the further question, "What constitutes wise and faithful stewardship?"

I shared with you last week that the phrase "good and faithful steward" was not applicable to David Shirey for the first 25 years of my life. My excuses included the fact that stewardship was not something my father ever taught me, and I was beset by misunderstandings that dampened my motivation to give. But I concluded last week's sermon by telling you I married a woman who was taught how and why to give by her parents. She taught me what they taught her which they had gleaned from the pages of scripture. Call it "giving by the book."

If you leaf through the pages of the Hebrew scriptures, there is one word that pops up again and again in regard to stewardship. Over thirty times it appears. It's that blessed "T" word: tithe. Tithe means one-tenth. As in one-tenth of my income to the Lord. In the Hebrew scriptures, the wise and faithful steward invariably tithes. Abraham comes home from battle laden with booty, runs smack dab into Melchizedek, priest of the Most High God, and in a fit of awe and reverence, gives him one-tenth (Genesis 14:20). Jacob is camped out at the foot of the legendary ladder leading up to heaven and promises God a tenth of all he has to his name (Genesis 28:20-22). Throughout Genesis, Exodus, Leviticus, Numbers, and Deuteronomy, the sacred books known as "the law," the tithe is the measure of wise and faithful stewardship.

Turn to the New Testament and stewardship takes on a different guise. Surprisingly enough, tithing is hardly mentioned in the New Testament. Jesus calls for more than a tithe. Abraham, Jacob, Moses and company gave their 10% and walked away with 90%, but when Jesus called his disciples "they left everything and followed him" (Luke 5:11). Jesus tells the rich ruler who inquired about being a disciple, "Sell all that you own and distribute the money to the poor, and you will have treasure in heaven; then come, follow me" (Luke 18:22). He walked away. Maybe if Jesus had only asked for a tithe, he would have had another disciple! In Acts 2:44, the early Christians "had all things in common." Not just 10%. Everything. And then there's Jesus' memorable words about the widow's offering: "All of them have contributed out of their abundance, but she out of her poverty has put in everything she had, all she had to live on" (Mark 12:44). Not a tithe. Everything.

What are we going to do? Depending on where we look in the Bible, we find a different perspective on what constitutes wise and faithful stewardship. Tithe. Everything to the poor. Share all things in common. Everything we have.

With all these different examples, how do we decide? Are there some guidelines we can use as we consider what to give?

I think so. Here are some principles for wise and faithful stewardship that honor the witness of the entirety of scripture.[6]

Beginning with the principle of priority. Wise and faithful stewardship puts God first. Moses told the people: "When you have come into the land that the Lord your God is giving you as an inheritance to possess and you possess it and settle in it, you shall take some of the first of all the fruit of the ground, which you harvest from the land that the Lord your God is giving you, and you shall put it in a basket and go to the place that the Lord your God will choose as a dwelling for his name" (Deuteronomy 26:2). Proverbs 3:9 says, "Honor the Lord with your substance and with the firstfruits of all your produce." The operative word is first.

The question is, "Do we give God firstfruits or leftovers? Is God our first thought or an afterthought?" I know if Jennie and I don't put God first in our finances — create our budget so that we give to God first — there are any number of others out there on our doorstep waiting to cut in and take God's rightful place at the head of line: Kentucky Utilities, Verizon, Time Warner, MasterCard, Kentucky American Water, and our mortgage holder. I know that if we didn't decide that as a matter of wise and faithful stewardship God comes first, they'd butt in line, take our firstfruits (not to mention our second, third, fourth and fifth fruits) and God would end up with the leftovers, if anything at all.

Billy Graham once said, "A checkbook is a theological document; it tells you who you are and what you worship." The principle of priority invites us to put our money where our mouth is. With our mouths we say Jesus Christ is Lord meaning he is #1 in our priorities. So, on the first day of the week, first thing in the morning, with the firstfruits of our income, in response to the first commandment, "You shall have no other gods before me," we put God first and give God "firstfruits" rather than leftovers. The principle of priority.

Next is the principle of proportionality. Deuteronomy 16:10 says, "You shall... contribute a freewill offering in proportion to the blessing that you have received from the Lord your God." The Bible presents as a guideline for giving a proportion as opposed to a specific amount. What's the wisdom in that? If everyone were called to give the same amount, it would hardly be fair. If people of greater and lesser means were called to give the same amount that wouldn't be right. Instead, the Bible invites all to give in equal measure — in proportion to what we have.

What proportion you may ask? As we've already noted, the earliest biblical standard is 10%. A tithe. A word that means one-tenth. God's people were told to "Set apart a tithe of all the yield of your seed that is brought in yearly from the field" (Deuteronomy 14:22). And then, "All tithes from the land, whether the seed from the ground or the fruit from the tree, are the Lord's; they are holy to the Lord" (Leviticus 27:30).

Depending on where you are now in your giving (I encourage you to do the math and see what percentage you give to God), 10% may seem like an imposing goal. Here's a suggestion: start at 2%, 4%, or 6% and grow from there year by year toward the tithe. Tithing is my personal practice with my wife — I would never invite you to do something the Bible doesn't call for or that I don't strive to practice myself.

When Jennie and I were first married, my check from my student church was $75 a week, which led to a check in the amount of $7.50. But when I went to my first full-time church and received a raise to $350 a week, I realized a tithe would be $35 — and I balked at writing a check for that much money!

That's when someone told me the story of a guy who asked his pastor to pray for God to bless his career and that in gratitude to God he would tithe the firstfruits of every pay check.

Years later, he made an appointment with the pastor.

"Pastor, he said, "When I first came to you my salary was $20,000 on which I tithed $2,000 each year. And each year when I received a raise, I tithed on that new amount. But now I've advanced in my career to the point my income is five times what I started off at and well, 10% of what I make now is a lot of money to give away. Do you understand where I'm coming from?"

The pastor said, "I sure do. Would you like me to pray for you?"

The man said, "I knew you'd understand."

Whereupon the pastor said, "Dear Lord, please reduce John's income to a level at which he'll feel comfortable tithing again."

It's the principle of proportionality. We give restaurant servers 15-20%. Surely God's service merits 5-10% less than that.

The principle of regularity is next. Writing to the Corinthians on an offering he is receiving, Paul tells them to "put aside" their gift "on the first day of every week" (1 Corinthians 16:1-3). The first day of every week means regularly. Regularly as opposed to haphazardly. Regularly as opposed to whenever I think about it or whenever I feel like it. Regularly as in every Sunday. Every month. Every year. When the crops are harvested. When the paycheck arrives. When you receive the commission.

Why the importance of regularity in giving thanks to God with our offerings? Well, how often does God bless us so as to occasion our thanksgiving? Sporadically? Occasionally? Once in a blue moon? No, God blesses us regularly. The verse from the great hymn says it all:

"Morning by morning new mercies I see.

All I have needed, thy hand has provided.
Great is thy faithfulness Lord until to me."[7]

In response to God's blessing us regularly, we give regularly.

For Jennie and me, offering envelopes long served as reminders of the principle of regularity. With the date of each and every Sunday printed on them, they were tangible reminders and invitations for us to be regular in our giving. Nowadays, automatic bank drafts ensure regularity.

For good and faithful stewards, the principles of priority, proportionality and regularity are seasoned with the principle of gratitude. Paul uses the word cheerful: "Each of you must give as you have made up your mind, not regretfully or under compulsion, for God loves a cheerful giver" (2 Corinthians 9:7).

The Greek word translated cheerful is hilaros from which we get our word hilarious. An elder in my Arizona church told me a story about a stewardship sermon he heard once. After the pastor expounded upon cheerful giving throughout his sermon, the offering plates were passed. As the plates reached a man who was not exactly known for a playful spirit or sense of humor, he dropped his envelope in the plate, threw up his arms and shouted, "Woohoo!"

People give out of all kinds of motivations — guilt and drear obligation being two of the inferior ones. It's cheerful giving born out of deep gratitude that spurs wise and faithful stewards' giving. Be a hilarious giver.

A few years ago, Jennie and I got a good, long laugh. We received a letter from the IRS informing us our tax return was being audited. Why our laughter? Because they were auditing us for the amount of charitable giving we claimed. They were not questioning us for giving too little to Uncle Sam, but for giving too much to God! Apparently tithing is a red flag to the IRS. It's suspect behavior giving away so much. That is subversive.

Well, count me a shameless subversive because I invite you to join Jennie and me on the IRS' list of dangerously cheerful givers — folks who have a record — a record of giving according to the principles of priority, proportionality, regularity, and gratitude. Fill out a pledge card and mail it to the church or fill out the form online. If you're not a member of our congregation, you're excused from this. I don't want to get you in trouble with the IRS, just my church family!

Jesus asks, "Who is the wise and faithful steward?"

I don't know about you, but, O Lord, I want to be in that number when the wise and faithful stewards come marchin' in.

Woohoo!

Pointers From Paul's Playbook

2 Corinthians 8:7-15

One of these days I'm going to preach a sermon on giving. I'm not ready to do it just yet. In fact, it will probably be quite a while before I preach my sermon on giving. But I know one thing for sure: when I do give my sermon on giving, I'll take my lead from Paul. Specifically, Paul's second letter to the Corinthians, chapters eight and nine. Those two chapters are some of the best commentaries on the whys and wherefores of giving in the entire Bible. There's plenty of food for thought there for someone like me who wants guidance on how to preach a sermon on giving.

And who couldn't use a little guidance on how to talk to people about giving? It's common knowledge that one of the things that turns a lot of people off about churches is "They're always asking for money." Have you heard that one before? I sure have. I've been around church circles long enough now to sense that the prospect of having to preach a sermon on giving (or having to listen to one) is not a happy thought. The way I look at it, when you're dealing with something that apparently causes as much anxiety as asking or being asked for money, only fools rush in where angels fear to tread. So, I'm going to hold off before I preach my sermon on giving. In the meantime, I'm going to see what I can learn from Paul.

For instance, I've learned from Paul's playbook that the word invite is of paramount importance. When Paul wrote to the folks in Corinth, he made it very clear he was not requiring them to make an offering. "I do not say this as a command" (2 Corinthians 8:8) is how he put it. Rather, he invited them to give "of their own free will" (2 Corinthians 8:3 RSV). In his words, "Each of you must give as you have made up your mind, not reluctantly or under compulsion, for God loves a cheerful giver" (2 Corinthians 9:7).

Given that, I've made a note to myself for when I do my sermon on giving. Invite. Do not pressure. Nobody responds well when they feel they're being strong-armed or manipulated or made to feel guilty. Even more so when the issue at hand is an offering. I've learned from Paul the word is "invite."

Then it dawned on me that the things we invite other people to do without hesitation are things we've found to be enjoyable ourselves. Right? Think of the things you gladly invite someone else to do. Go to the game. See that movie that just came out. Check out the street fair. Go to that restaurant with the great pasta and fresh bread. The things we invite others to do are things we've found to be personally satisfying or worthwhile ourselves or at least they promise to be.

Paul is a case in point. The offering he invited the Corinthians to give to was clearly dear to his heart. He believed wholeheartedly in the cause it would support, so he had no qualms about inviting others to join in.

What was the cause Paul felt so strongly about? The offering was for the church in Jerusalem. The Jerusalem church was the mother church of all churches. Jerusalem is where it all began with Jesus' crucifixion and the word of his resurrection. It was in Jerusalem on the Day of Pentecost that the church was born. Now there had been some friction between Paul and the leaders of the Jerusalem church, Peter and James, over the issue of integrating Gentiles into the church. (What church hasn't had its share of theological head butting?) But as far as Paul was concerned, the strained relationship only made the offering more significant. Yes, people in Jerusalem were suffering due to economic hardship, cause enough for an offering to support them, but Paul also saw the offering as an opportunity to mend fences as well. With the offering, Paul and the Gentile Christians would be extending an olive branch to their theological opponents. In other words, far from trying to coax out of people enough cash to underwrite next year's budget, Paul was inviting an offering that would relieve suffering, promote reconciliation, and underscore the unity of the church. With those noble ends in mind, no wonder Paul was so enthusiastic about inviting others to dig deeply and give generously.

Given that example, I've made a note for when I do my sermon on giving: highlight the ways in which the offering will relieve human suffering, bring people together, and show forth the worldwide embrace of the church's arms. It's when somebody stands up there and asks for people to please give because it costs money to keep the lights on and the air conditioner running (not to mention doing your fair share to keep those seven till midnight committee meetings going strong) that people begin to shift in their seats and look for the exits. My experience has been that once people see that their offerings are making a genuine difference in other peoples' lives, they actually want to give.

That was Paul's experience with the Macedonian Christians. They were in no position to make an offering. Far from it. But even though they were experiencing "extreme poverty" themselves, they responded with an offering which "overflowed in a wealth of generosity" (2 Corinthians 8:2). Now you tell me — What calls forth that kind of generosity? Not cajoling from the pulpit. Not pummeling people's ears with left-right combinations of "ought" and "should." My sense is that the Macedonians simply "got it." They knew deep down that making an offering doesn't empty your pocket as much as it fills your heart with the unspeakable pleasure that comes with joining God in making a tangible difference in the lives of other human beings. The Macedonians got it and gave it. In "a wealth of generosity" no less.

I've made a note in my "Sermon on Giving" file to make sure and give examples of people I know who have come to the point that they give generously and joyfully and actually look forward to giving. Paul used the example of the Macedonians. I've got in my memory bank several people (unlikely benefactors if all you looked at was the status of their bank account) whose giving "overflowed in a wealth of generosity," people who when I asked them "Why?" said basically the same thing: they knew of nothing more satisfying than giving.

Just the other day I read in the paper about a guy who made that discovery a few years ago and hasn't ever gotten over it. The reporter said one Thanksgiving the guy was looking for something more sustaining than feasts and football, so he got out a map and headed south. Where he lived in Arizona, south means Mexico. He crossed the border and found a woman cooking tamales over a burning tire for a bunch of kids playing in the dirt. She had found them living in junk cars and eating out of garbage cans. She took them in and started an orphanage of sorts. The guy from Phoenix decided then and there to take up an offering for her, an offering that over the years has helped build dormitories, a soup kitchen, a clinic, and who knows what else.

Do you know what that guy told the reporter he has discovered through all this? "The more time you spend on yourself," he said, "the more self-absorbed and the less happy you are. The more time spent in service of others, the happier you are."

"Happiness," he said, "is tied to a more luxurious heart."

I've made a note to myself that when I give my sermon on giving, I need to tell about people like that guy who, contrary to the acquisitive fever that infects our culture, aspires above all else to a higher standard of giving. People like him have discovered a fundamental truth about life in Christ that I know to be true. That is: there is a large part of us that can only be filled as we empty ourselves. In giving our lives away, we find life like we've never known it before.

Of course, my sermon on giving wouldn't be complete unless I point out what is at the very heart of all giving. Paul reminded me of what that is when he told the Corinthians that when someone makes an offering from the heart, he or she is above all else mirroring what Jesus did. In its purest form, an offering is an embodiment of Jesus' self-giving love.

What Gave Giving A Bad Name?

Are you familiar with those bracelets with the letters WWJD? What would Jesus do? Well, when it comes to deciding whether or not to make an offering or how much of one to make, what do you think Jesus would do? Paul said of Jesus, "Though he was rich, for your sakes he became poor, so that by his poverty you might became rich" (2 Corinthians 8:9). Elsewhere Paul wrote, he "emptied himself, taking the form of a slave" (Philippians 2:7). Jesus emptied not just his pockets, but his life. He poured it out for us so that we might be filled. That's how it is Paul can say that when we give generously of ourselves, we do what Jesus did.

In that light, how striking it was for me to discover that the word Paul uses to refer to the offering — the word that gets translated "this generous undertaking" (2 Corinthians 8:6-7,19) — is the Greek word charis. Grace. In a word, an offering is pure grace.

You can bet I'll add that insight to the file I'm keeping for my upcoming sermon on giving. I'll stick it in there right next to all the other pointers I've learned from Paul's playbook. Things like:

- Invite. Don't command, strong-arm, or plead.
- Show how the offering will relieve suffering, help reconcile a broken world, and show forth the wide embrace of God's love instead of just oiling the ecclesiastical machine.
- Tell stories of people who have made the life-changing discovery that in emptying ourselves, we are filled.
- Ask, 'What would Jesus do?' and remind everyone of Jesus' example.
- Tell how the word translated "generous undertaking" is really the word "grace."

That's the last entry I have in my file for my upcoming sermon on giving. When all is said and done, remind them that giving is pure grace.

Someday, I'm going to preach a sermon on the grace of giving. And when I do, you can bet I'll let you know in advance.

A Most Delicate Issue

Mark 12:38-44

An issue has been brought to my attention this week that needs to be addressed. Since it is a most delicate issue, it will require wisdom and sensitivity, so I thought I would ask Chuck, today's worship leader, to take it into his capable hands.

But Chuck could rightly say, "David, this is an issue that deserves the attention of the elders. I think you ought to talk with Deanne about this one. She's the chair of the elders."

But Deanne could say, "David, since this is a stewardship issue, how about going to Ray first? He chairs stewardship and finance. See what he thinks."

This being Ray's very first year, though, and this being a matter of strict confidentiality — a person's giving record — Ray could rightly direct me to Susan, our treasurer. Susan handles all such issues with unquestioned competence and integrity. She'd know what to do.

But I got to thinking, this is exactly the kind of issue that would make a good learning experience for Kory, our student pastoral intern. I could say, "Kory, let's say you're the pastor of a congregation, and let's say this issue arises. I can hear him now — "David, I think I'd approach Chuck or Deanne or Ray or Susan...."

Enough beating around the bush. Here's the issue. The late Gordon Cosby, founding pastor of Church of the Savior in Washington, DC, told of when he was a young man in the late 1930s and was the minister of a small congregation in Virginia. As he told it:

"My deacon sent for me one day and told me that he wanted my help. 'We have in our congregation,' he said, 'a widow with six children. I have looked at the records and discovered that she is putting into the treasury of the church each month $4.00

— a tithe of her income. Of course, she is unable to do this. We want you to go and talk to her and let her know that she needs to feel no obligation whatsoever and free her from the responsibility.'"[8]

Now what I want to know is who is going to go and talk to this poor widow? Chuck? Deanne? Ray? Susan? Kory?

Mark told us Jesus "sat down opposite the treasury and watched the crowd putting money into the treasury" (Mark 12:41). Around one of the courtyards in front of the Jerusalem temple were placed thirteen trumpet-shaped containers into which people deposited their offerings. Now I don't know about you, but just the thought of Jesus sitting and watching as I make my offering is enough to give me pause. I mean, I've been in ministry long enough to know how tightly congregations guard the confidentiality of people's giving. We don't want anyone else to know what we give, and I suspect we'd prefer that Jesus not know either!

Last week at a statewide assembly of our churches, an offering was taken. I don't remember whether it was for the establishment of new churches or our mission work in Nepal, but Jennie handed our eight-year-old daughter Laura a bill to place in the offering plate as it floated down our pew. I won't tell you what it was — it's none of your business. And what did Laura do? She unfolded that bill, then promptly hoisted it high above her head, angling it toward the light as if she was looking for the imbedded watermark to shine through. All the while, she was allowing the people on both sides of us and in the pews behind us to see exactly what it was we were giving. And tilting it heavenward like she did, I don't doubt for a moment that even God and Jesus could see our offering!

At any rate, Mark told us Jesus sat and watched the crowd putting money into the treasury. "A poor widow came and put in two small copper coins" (Matthew 12:42). In the King James Version of the Bible they are referred to as "mites." In Greek, they were called lepta (singular: lepton), a word that literally means "a tiny thing" — which they were. They were the smallest coins in circulation at the time, with a value less than our penny.

An aside: they're still around. In fact, I came across an advertisement on the internet years back for Guy Clark's Ancient Coins and Antiquities in which I found item SP101 The Widow's Mite. The ad read in part, "The so-called widow's mite is one of the most popular ancient coins — not because of its great beauty as a coin, but because of what it represents." The ad then went on to retell this morning's scripture passage, concluding with a listed retail price at that time of $15.00 and these words in italics: These make great unique gifts for that person who has most everything or for a pastor or Sunday school teacher.

Back to the story: What Jesus observed was a poor widow placing her last two copper coins in the temple treasury. Whereupon Jesus called his disciples and said, "Truly I tell you, this poor widow has put in more than all those who are contributing to the treasury. For all of them have contributed out of their abundance" (including the mortified couple whose little girl is holding up that bill to the sunlight), "but she out of her poverty has put in everything she had, all she had to live on" (Matthew 12:43, 44). Plink. Plink.

Now, my question is the question the deacon in Gordon Cosby's church approached him with, "Who's going to go and talk with her? She's unable to do that. Who's going to go and talk to her and let her know that she needs to feel no obligation whatsoever and free her from the responsibility?"

I can think of several approaches.

For instance, she could be told the temple doesn't need her offering. Let's be honest. In the larger scope of things, are her two mites really going to make that much of a difference? Thirteen offering receptacles in the temple, each filled with thousands of coins. Her two mites amount to 2/1000ths of 1/13th. Trust my ballpark math. Her offering is 2/13,000ths of the temple budget. Less than a thousandth of a percent. What she had to offer pales in comparison to what others can give.

Maybe that same logic has crossed your mind. I know that you don't know what others in this church give. But then again, you know. You've looked around and imagined and the thought has crossed your mind that what you give compared what they give must be a very, very small percentage; so small, in fact, that if you didn't give what you give it wouldn't make the slightest difference in the budget. Would somebody who understands that please kindly tell the poor widow over yonder that the temple really doesn't need her offering as much as she does?

If she doesn't respond to that, how about this fact? Tell her that the temple really doesn't need her offering. I mean need in terms of deserve. Somebody tell that widow that in the paragraph immediately preceding her offering Jesus had lambasted the entire temple culture. That included the building, which had become an end in itself (a phenomenon some wag called "the edifice complex") and the religious establishment, who had become more caught up in pomp and circumstance than humility and servanthood. In Jesus words, "Beware of the scribes, who like to walk around in long robes and to be greeted with respect in the marketplaces and to have the best seats in the synagogues and places of honor at banquets!" (Matthew 12:38-39). The whole shebang had become corrupt to the point that Jesus said, "They devour widows' houses" (Matthew 12:40). Somebody go tell that poor widow that whereas her two mites might help provide a simple thatched roof over her gray head, she's giving her last two cents to a building that's already paid off and to scribes whose long robes have been paid for by widows' offerings. She shouldn't be taking up an offering for them! Why, they ought to be taking up an offering for her! Somebody go tell her that that's just not right, that giving money to institutional religion the way it is these days is just throwing money down the drain. And tell her Jesus said so in Mark 12:38-40.

And if she doesn't respond to that, well at least you might suggest that she cut her giving in half. I mean, instead of two mites, have her give one. One for the church, one for her – 50%

of all she has is five times a tithe. A quintuple tithe! Who ever heard of giving 50% to the Lord?

Being an old widow, though, she probably knows the old favorite hymns by heart, like "Take my life, and let it be consecrated, Lord to thee. Take my silver and my gold, not a mite would I withhold."[9] But tell her that's just a figure of speech. We're to withhold mites for ourselves after all, several of them, in fact, so as to provide for ourselves creature comforts and something special every now and again.

She probably also knows "When I survey the wondrous cross on which the prince of glory died... All the vain things that charm me most I sacrifice them to his blood." That's the one that ends, "Love so amazing, so divine, demands my soul, my life, my all."[10] But tell her the reason all was chosen was that it rhymes with small. If the hymn writer could have found something to rhyme with "a little bit" he would have! All is too much!

But she probably knows scripture, too, including Paul's writing to the Corinthians about the Christians in Macedonia. "Their extreme poverty... overflowed in a wealth of generosity on their part. ...They voluntarily gave according to their means and even beyond their means" (2 Corinthians 8:2-3). She'd probably say that if they gave out of their poverty, she could certainly give out of hers!

She probably even knew that following this story, Mark's gospel turns toward the cross. This teaching ends Chapter 12. In Chapter 13, Jesus spoke of the end. In Chapters 14 and 15, he was crucified. She might say, "Jesus gave his all, didn't he? Why shouldn't his followers?"

I don't know how to answer that one. But somebody needs to go tell her that she really doesn't need to give anything and really shouldn't give anything to long-robed, long-winded preachers in towering temples, but if she insists on giving something one mite is plenty. Would somebody go and talk some sense into that woman? Chuck? Deanne? Ray? Susan? Kory?

Well, you're off the hook. I will have you know that one brave soul volunteered to go on behalf of the church and speak to the poor widow. Pastor Cosby went. Bless his heart, at the behest of the deacon who told him of the widowed mother of six who was tithing her income at the rate of $4.00 a week, Pastor Cosby went out to make a call.

In his words, "I went and told her of the concern of the deacons. I told her as graciously and as supportively as I know how that she was relieved of the responsibility of giving."

Good for him! Somebody needed to do it.

But wait, there's more: "As I talked with her the tears came into her eyes. 'I want to tell you,' she said, 'that you are taking away the last thing that gives my life dignity and meaning.'"

My, my, my. You know what I think? I think our thinking that somebody needs to talk her out of that offering says more about our view of offerings than it does about hers. Apparently for her, the giving of an offering to God is not an onerous obligation to be dutifully and drudgingly done, but a precious pleasure to be joyfully embraced. What were her words? "I want to tell you that you are taking away the last thing that gives my life dignity and meaning."

I need to confess something. Up until this week, I had in my mind an image of that woman as aged, wrinkled. Beleaguered by the adversity life has unfairly dealt her, I imagined her shuffling up to the offering receptacles, stoop-shouldered and downcast so as to fulfill her religious obligation of making an offering. Poor lady.

But no longer do I think of her that way. This week I saw her in my mind's eye, upright, proud, her eyes filled with life, her visage radiant with joy. She strides across the temple courtyard to the offering receptacles, drops her two mites into the receptacles, lifts her head skyward, her countenance beaming.

I think maybe we ought to just leave that woman alone. Better yet, I think she should come and talk to us about giving. Don't you think? Chuck? Deanne? Ray? Susan? Kory? Is there somebody here who'd be willing to contact her and invite her to come and talk to us about stewardship? I don't know about you, but I want what she has. How she lives. How she gives.

The Macedonian Miracle

2 Corinthians 8:1-7

There are all kinds of miracles in the Bible: Red Sea parting, walls of Jericho falling down, water turning into wine, and lepers' skin made smooth as babies' bottoms. But I submit to you that right up there with all those miracles is what Paul witnessed at the church in Macedonia where Paul says they begged to take part in a stewardship campaign. In his words, "I can testify they voluntarily gave according to their means, and even beyond their means, begging us earnestly for the privilege of sharing in this ministry" (2 Corinthians 8:4). As one who has undertaken his share of stewardship campaigns over four decades of ministry, that beats anything I've ever heard of. People begging for the privilege of making a pledge? Pu-leeze!

I know what really happened. Word got out that Paul was on the prowl and folks were saying, "If the phone rings and the caller ID says Paul, don't answer it! Let the answering machine pick up." They were saying, "If you get a letter in the mail in November on church stationery from Pastor Paul, don't open it! It's got a pledge card in it. Drop it in the recycling unopened. Say you never saw it." People were forwarding an email to one another that had as its heading the word Warning! It read: "If you get an email with the words Paul, church, or stewardship in the title, delete it immediately. Don't open it. It will harm your computer, savings account, and stock portfolio, and has even been known to crack children's piggy banks down the middle."

People don't beg for the favor of taking part in stewardship campaigns! They beg to be spared from them. Yet, the folks in Macedonia begged for the privilege of taking part.

That was a miracle on several counts. For instance, they gave even though they were living in trying economic circumstances. "During a severe ordeal of affliction," Paul wrote, "their extreme poverty overflowed in a wealth of generosity" (2 Corinthians 8:2). Folks who really didn't have much to give gave something anyway. Diminished income didn't restrict generous outgo. That's a miracle.

But there's more: they gave sacrificially. Paul testified, "They voluntarily gave according to their means, and even beyond their means" (2 Corinthians 8:3). They went the second mile. They gave beyond what any reasonable person could have expected. That's miraculous. Plus, Paul noted "their abundant joy" (2 Corinthians 8:2). They didn't give begrudgingly, but joyfully. It's later in this chapter Paul pens the famous line, "God loves a cheerful giver" (2 Corinthians 9:6).

In sum: those Macedonian Christians living in hard times nevertheless gave generously, even sacrificially and cheerfully. Miraculous stuff! Which got me to wondering. How'd they do that? What happened in Macedonia to precipitate such a miracle of generous giving in such hard times?

According to Paul, the key was this: "They gave themselves first to the Lord" (2 Corinthians 8:5). They didn't first call in a professional fundraiser. They didn't first do a needs assessment. They didn't first do a potential lead donor income analysis. None of the above. First, they gave themselves to the Lord. The Macedonian miracle was the fruit of a congregation who put God first. Everything followed from that.

Martin Luther said, "There are three conversions necessary: the conversion of the heart, the mind, and the purse." The order is right: First must come the conversion of the heart. First, I give myself to the Lord. A hymn sings, "Take my life, and let it be consecrated, Lord, to thee. " When we give our lives, everything else follows, including the subsequent verses of the hymn:

"Take my hands, and let them move
at the impulse of thy love.
Take my will, and make it thine; it shall be no longer mine.
Take my intellect, and use
every power as thou shalt choose.
Take myself, and I will be ever, only, all for thee."[11]

It's as Jesus said, "Strive first for the kingdom of God and his righteousness, and all these things will be given to you as well" (Matthew 6:33). Put God first and the giving of everything else gladly follows. Extraordinary things happen. People count it a privilege to contribute to a stewardship campaign and actually beg to take part.

Speaking of the extraordinary things that happen when people in a church give themselves first to God, I'll never forget the story a colleague of mine, the late Reverend Doctor Ben Gerardy, told me years ago about a church in western Kansas where almost everyone is involved in raising wheat. One day the church treasurer resigned her position and everyone wondered what was going to happen to the church. She had been the treasurer for years and the church had appreciated all her hard and dedicated work, but the day she resigned everybody began to wonder, "Who's going to do that work for the church now?"

Finally, the church officers asked the manager of the local grain elevator if he would be willing to serve as the new treasurer of the church. He agreed to do so, but only on two conditions. First, the congregation had to agree that no treasurer's report be given during the first year he served as treasurer. Second, no questions would be asked about the finances of the church during that year.

The people were a bit taken aback by his request, but since no one else was willing to serve in the capacity of treasurer and what's more, since most of those wheat farmers did business with him at his grain elevator on a regular basis and trusted him, they agreed to his conditions and allowed him to proceed as treasurer.

That year, everything at the church seemed to be going great. No one was worried about the finances since everything seemed to be going fine. Finally, however, at the end of the year it was time for the yearly congregational meeting. All of the business items and the elections took place as expected and everyone was very, very pleased with the ongoing ministry of the church.

Finally, it was time for the year-end financial report. The treasurer stood up an gave the following report:

"Outreach giving has been paid over 200% more than the previous year. Our programs of faith formation for children, youth, and adults are fully underwritten with room for expansion. We have such a surplus in our operating budget we're able to fully underwrite an additional mission trip this summer. There are no outstanding bills and the cash balance is 20% more than it has ever been. The church's mortgage has been paid in full."

"How is all that possible?" someone asked. "Where did all that money come from?" "What did you do? Rob a bank?"

The treasurer then quietly answered: "All of you bring your grain to my grain elevator. Throughout the year, I simply withheld 10% on your behalf and gave it to the church in your name. You didn't even miss it."

Do you see what happens when we give the firstfruits of our fields to God who owns it all but entrusts it to us to use in ways that honor God and bless others?"

This is all to say that whether it's a church in western Kansas or in Bible-times Macedonia, miracles happen when God's people "first give themselves to the Lord." After Paul wrote of the Macedonian miracle — people begging for the privilege of taking part in giving, and then giving sacrificially and joyfully — he concluded by writing, "Now as you excel in everything — in faith, in speech, in knowledge, in utmost eagerness, and in our love for you — so we want you to excel also in this generous undertaking" (2 Corinthians 8:7).

Hey, the way I look at it is this: If the Red Sea can part and the walls of Jericho can come a tumblin' down, if water can be turned into wine and lepers be restored, if miracles can happen in Macedonia and Kansas, why not in downtown Lexington?

May God help us excel in the grace of giving.

Something Beautiful For God

Mark 14:3-9

We're in rarified air this morning. Before us is one of just a handful of incidents in Jesus' ministry that caused him to shake his head in wonder at what happened. Usually, it's us who are doing the oohing and aahing at what Jesus did. But this story suggests there are things we human beings do that cause Jesus to gush. I know of four instances in the course of Jesus' ministry when somebody did something so remarkable it stopped Jesus in his tracks and evoked his praise.

On one occasion, a centurion whose servant was paralyzed came and asked Jesus if he would please come to his ailing servant's side. That Roman army officer was so humbled in Jesus' presence that he said "Lord, I am not worthy to have you come under my roof, but only speak the word, and my servant will be healed" (Matthew 8:8). Jesus was so taken by the man's faith and humility he said, "Truly I tell you, in no one in Israel have I found such faith" (Matthew 8:10). High praise.

On another occasion, Jesus was sitting with his disciples in the temple, watching people as they made their offerings (Jesus watches us as we make our offerings? Yikes). A widow walked up and dropped in two copper coins, whereupon Jesus got his disciples' attention and said, "Truly I tell you, this poor widow has put in more than all those who are contributing to the treasury. For all of them have contributed out of their abundance, but she out of her poverty has put in everything she had, all she had to live on" (Mark 12:43-44). That's high praise, too.

When in response to Jesus' question, "Who do people say that I am?" Peter said, "You are the Messiah, the Son of the Living God," Jesus exclaimed, "Blessed are you, Simon bar Jonah! For flesh and blood has not revealed this to you but my

Father in heaven" (Matthew 16:16, 17). High praise.

Then this: an unnamed woman entered a home where Jesus was eating. She broke open a flask of expensive perfume and poured it over Jesus' head. In response to what she did, Jesus said, "She has performed a good service for me" (Mark 14:6). The New International Version has, "She has done a beautiful thing to me." Then Jesus added, "Truly I tell you, wherever the good news is proclaimed in the whole world, what she has done will be told in remembrance of her" (Mark 14:9).

"She has done a beautiful thing." What did she do?

One explanation is that what she did in breaking open that flask and pouring its contents on Jesus' head was to make her confession of faith in him. How so? The word Messiah is the Hebrew word that means, "the anointed one." The Greek word for "the anointed one" is Christos. Christ. Earthly kings in ancient Israel were anointed meaning a flask of oil was opened and ceremonially poured over their heads as a visible symbol of God's Spirit and favor covering them from head to toe (2 Kings 9:1-13; 1 Samuel 10:1). So, when the woman anointed Jesus' head with the perfume, she was saying, "You are the King of kings. The Messiah. The Christ." That Jesus responded to what she did by saying "Beautiful" suggests that yet today whenever someone makes a confession of faith by pouring out not perfume but the words, "I believe that Jesus is the Christ" causes our Lord to rejoice and say, "That's a beautiful thing."

I believe Jesus was moved as well because her offering was sacrificial. Like that widow in the temple who gave everything she had (two copper coins), this woman gave Jesus everything she had, an alabaster jar filled with expensive perfume. In Mark's words, "While he was at Bethany in the house of Simon the leper, as he sat at the table, a woman came with an alabaster jar of very costly ointment of nard" (Mark 14:3). How costly? One of the men who scolded her said it "could have been sold for more than 300 denarii" (Mark 14:5). How much is that? Three hundred denarii were equivalent to a year's wages for a laborer. Go ahead and translate that number into your salary.

Now imagine breaking open your piggy bank and in one fell swoop making an offering totaling a full year's pay checks. That's some offering! Beautiful.

But even more than the amount she gave was the way in which she gave it. Mark said she "broke open the jar and poured the ointment on his head" (Mark 14:3). That word translated broke is the same word used in Exodus to describe what Moses did to the stone tablets when he came down from Mt. Sinai and saw the people of Israel worshiping the golden calf.[12] He broke them all right — he smashed them to smithereens. So did the unnamed woman in this story smash open her flask before emptying out its contents on Jesus' head. Meaning what? Meaning she gave with reckless abandon. Meaning she was an extravagant giver. Talk about throwing caution to the wind! Talk about pulling out all the stops! She smashed that flask and poured out its precious contents — every last drop.

What a contrast to the giving that was expected in those days. What was expected back then — the socially acceptable thing to do — was for the host of a party to drop a few drops of perfume onto the head of a guest when he or she arrived. Drop. Drop. Drop. Three drops is enough. It strikes me that "three drops is enough" pretty well describes how we're conditioned to give in our society as well. Am I right? We carefully calculate what we have, do a quick calculation of what would be about right, what is reasonable, what is our fair share, and then, holding the medicine dropper just so, we measure out one, two, three drops. There, that's enough. By contrast, here's a woman who smashes all expectations and pours out everything she has. Jesus, who is accustomed to receiving offerings drop by drop, sits there dumbfounded, awestruck, and says, "Beautiful. She has done a beautiful thing to me."

Is it any wonder Jesus recognizes extravagant giving when he sees it? God, after all, is the extravagant giver par excellence. When God created the heavens and the earth, did God do it with a medicine dropper mentality? "How many stars should I spring for in the night sky? How about three? Drop, drop, drop.

How many different species of birds ought I paint into the blue, blue sky? Three ought to be enough. Drop, drop, drop." Need I continue? God doesn't give drop, drop, drop. To the contrary! God is an extravagant giver and invites us to be extravagant givers, too. Why, when God entered history in the person of Jesus of Nazareth in order to bless, teach, heal, redeem, and save us, God didn't measure out grace with an eyedropper. Heavens, no! As the most beloved passage of all reminds us, "God so loved the world that God gave..." (John 3:16). Love gives; divine love gives extravagantly. Paul says, "Jesus emptied himself" (Philippians 2:7). He emptied his hands, his pockets, his heart, his very life. God is an extravagant giver and invites us to be extravagant givers, too. Jesus broke open the flask of his life and poured it all out for all of us. No wonder when he saw that woman smash her flask and pour out every last drop, he exclaimed, "Beautiful!"

Speaking of extravagant giving, the woman's gift was not well received by everyone. "Some were there," Mark told us, "who said to one another in anger, 'Why was the ointment wasted in this way? For this ointment could have been sold for more than three hundred denarii and the money given to the poor'" (Mark 14:5). I still hear that. "That congregation spent six figures on refurbishing their sanctuary. Couldn't it have been sunk into some social justice?" "Do you know how much went into that stained glass? Probably 300 denarii or more! If you could see out those windows, you'd see hungry people who need food."

But listen: What did Jesus say to those disparaging the woman's extravagant gift? "Leave her alone. Why are you bothering her? She has done a beautiful thing to me. The poor you will always have with you, and you can help them any time you want. But you will not always have me" (Mark 14:6, 7). Some take Jesus' words, "You will always have the poor with you," as an excuse for not doing anything for the poor. After all, they'll always be around. We'll never solve poverty. But that's not what Jesus meant. In his letters from prison, Dietrich

Bonhoeffer called Jesus "the man for others." He was always reaching out to the impoverished, excluded, and neglected. When Jesus shushed those who would have prevented the woman's pouring herself out for him, I think he was saying pouring oneself out by offering something for God and pouring oneself out by offering something for others are not mutually exclusive choices, but ought to go hand-in-hand. Disciples of Christ ought to pour ourselves out in offering lavish worship and overflowing grocery bags. We ought to provide a beautiful place for people to worship and affordable housing for all. We can pour ourselves out in love for God and in seeking justice for neighbors near and far. The book of Exodus is 50% (twenty chapters) God hearing the cries of slaves – extravagant outreach — and 50% (twenty chapters) instructions on building a tabernacle constructed of finest wood and precious gems — extravagant worship. Worship and mission, beautiful building and bountiful service, exquisite music and a passion for mercy and justice are not mutually exclusive in scripture. They're both called for and welcomed by God. We're called to pour ourselves out in service and worship.

I ask you: is there not something beautiful about sacrifice? There's something about one life freely choosing to pour itself out on behalf of another that is a breathtakingly beautiful thing to behold. I was thinking about that perfume poured out over Jesus' head and I imagined the fragrance that must have filled that entire room and wafted out into the streets. Passersby oblivious to what had happened would have caught a whiff and been brought up short in their tracks.

One asks, "What's that smell?"

Another says, "I don't know. Something beautiful, though."

And I say, "Darn right it's something beautiful! It's the sweet smell of sacrifice. It's one person pouring her life out upon the one who's poised to pour out his life for us all!" That brings to mind Paul's words to the Corinthians when he said, "Thanks be to God, who in Christ always leads us in triumphal procession and through us spreads in every place the fragrance that comes from knowing him. For we are the aroma of Christ to God among those who are being saved...a fragrance from life to life" (2 Corinthians 2:14-16). How about that? Paul describes the lives of extravagant givers who follow the lead of the one who poured himself out for all as a pleasant fragrance, a pleasing aroma. It's the sweet smell of sacrifice.

I say all this because we're invited next week to give of ourselves time, talent, and treasure to our congregation's ministries in the coming year. I'm mindful of the adage that has circulated through stewardship campaigns for many years, namely, "Not equal gifts, but equal sacrifice." We're invited by our Lord to aspire beyond a drop, drop, drop offering to pour out a sacrificial gift, something beautiful for God. As we do, remember the gift made by that unnamed woman, the one of whom Jesus said, "She has done a beautiful thing to me. Truly I tell you, wherever the good news is proclaimed in the whole world, what she has done will be told in remembrance of her" (Mark 14:6. 9).

Those are some sweet-smelling words. Amen and Amen.

Holy Choices

Joshua 24:1-8, 13-22

All sorts of jokes have been made about the topic of churches and preachers asking for money. I think I've heard them all.

Hey Preacher, did you hear the one about the two men who were stranded on a deserted island? One was cheerful. The other was downcast.

"Why are you so happy?" the one asked the other. "Don't you know we'll never be found? We're going to die on this god-forsaken place."

"Cheer up," his friend said, "We'll be fine. My church pledge is due next week and I know the Stewardship and Finance committee will find me."

I like a good joke, but don't count me in the Spare Me From The Stewardship Campaign Society. I welcome the opportunity to reflect on the word stewardship and its cardinal virtue of generosity.

After all, we were made by a generous God to be generous people. Generosity is in our DNA. Generous is what we are at our core. Years ago, someone pointed out to me the similarity between the words generous and genus. Do you recognize that word genus from ninth grade biology class? Back then, we learned every living organism can be classified according to Kingdom, Phylum, Class, Order, Family, Genus, and Species. Human beings are Kingdom: Animalia; Phylum: Chordata; Class: Mammalia; Order: Primates; Family: Hominidae; Genus: Homo; Species: Sapiens. The words generous and genus have the same root. Our genus as human beings is generosity. Generous is what God made us to be. When we're not generous, when we're stingy or miserly, when we're party to injustice, turning in on ourselves and turning away from others, it is corrupting of our true selves. That is not who we are.

We were created in the image of God, and God is the extravagant giver par excellence. John 3:16 begins, "God so loved the world, God gave." Love gives. Divine love gives extravagantly. Our genus, our birthright as God's own, is generosity.

Two members of our congregation attended a conference on the arts and worship several weeks ago. John told me he learned Vincent Van Gogh was a devout Christian and you can see it in his paintings. I asked him what he saw and he said, "Look closely at his brushstrokes. The man used gobs of paint. Starry Night has blues in thick, bounteous helpings. How much gold paint did he splurge on Sunflowers? Look at the purple paint used in thick abundance in irises. Why so much paint in depicting creation? Because Van Gogh saw that God spared no expense in creating this world so neither would he. Overly generous in his use of paint, he was paying homage to God's extravagant generosity."

Great observation, John! You're absolutely right. When God created the heavens and the earth, was God stingy? Did God say, "Let's see. One thoroughbred foal per bluegrass hillside is plenty." Did God say, "I'm not going to spend too much time carving out that canyon in northern Arizona. They can call it The Mediocre Canyon. That's good enough." Did God say, "Spices? Two is plenty. Salt and pepper. Flowers? Unnecessary frills. Colors? How many can I afford? People? I'll make one kind. They won't appreciate the differences anyway!" Does God scrimp? Clutch? Withhold? To the contrary, God is an extravagant giver and invites us to be extravagant givers, too.

Our scripture from Joshua underscores the fact that living a life marked by generosity is a choice we make (or don't). "Choose this day," Joshua says (Joshua 24:15). We have some holy choices to make in life and whether or not to be generous is one of them.

In terms of the stewardship of our lives, how do we choose to spend them? Somebody said there are two types of people in this world — givers and takers. God created us and Jesus redeemed us so that we might choose to be gracious givers — generous people.

In terms of the stewardship of our financial resources — we have several choices: spend it, save it, invest it, or give it. Each of those choices open into still more choices. Where do we spend our money and on what? How much do we save? What do we invest in? To whom do we give money and how much? Choices, choices, choices.

But the bottom line is this: the choice of how we spend our lives — as givers or takers — and the choice of how we spend, save, invest and give of our money is the fruit (sweet or sour) of one fundamental choice: Whom shall we serve? That's the ultimate question. Answer that question and live out its implications and all else follows.

Joshua knew that choices are important. Many choices don't really matter. What flavor toothpaste? Do I take route A or route B to get to church? Boxers or briefs? But then again, some choices have lasting...and everlasting effects. Somebody said that of all the things parents teach children, the most important thing a child needs to learn is how to make good choices. You can feed them, clothe them, educate them, and get them in every extracurricular activity under the sun, but if you don't teach a young person how to make good choices — to look at possible consequences before leaping to a decision — you're guilty of negligence in the first degree. So it is that Papa Joshua is talking to the children of Israel in one of his last addresses to them. He presses them to make the choice that undergirds all choices, the most important choice any of us ever make: Whom will you serve? Back in the late seventies when Bob Dylan was exploring Christianity, he wrote a song called "Gotta Serve Somebody."[13] He sang about having to serve somebody whether it be the devil or the Lord, then a gospel choir comes in, singing, "serve somebody!" Ol' Bob has a quirky, nasal voice, but a spot on theology: we're going to have to serve somebody. We can serve ourselves, someone else, some ideology or cause. We all have to answer the question: Whom will you serve?

It's interesting where Joshua takes the people to ask them that big question: Shechem. "Joshua gathered all the tribes of Israel to Shechem, and summoned the elders, the heads, the judges, and the officers of Israel; and they presented themselves before God" (Joshua 24:1). Do you know the significance of Shechem? That was the place where 800 years earlier God made the covenant with Abraham and Sarah. "In you all the families of the earth shall be blessed" (Genesis 12:3). Shechem was the place where it all began, where God's people first heard the good news of God's love for them and for the whole world, the place where they first chose for God. 800 years later, Joshua took them back to where it all began to invite them to rededicate themselves. To choose again.

Where's your Shechem? Where's the place where you first heard the good news of the gospel to the point you said, "I choose to serve God through Jesus Christ"? It hasn't been 800 years for any of us, but for some of us it's been decades since we first confessed our faith. Go back in your minds to your Shechem and give thanks for that place and those people who invited you to choose for the first time.

As for me and my house, I'm back in the baptistery of Central Christian Church (Disciples of Christ) in Warren, Ohio. It's Palm Sunday, 1972. I'm waiting in line to be baptized and I'm wondering how long Rev. Cox is going to hold Barbie Gibbons under the water because I'm next. When he finished baptizing her and extended his hands to me, I walked down into the baptistery. As I did, I heard someone blow their nose in the congregation and without even looking I knew it was my grandfather. He was crying, blowing his nose, and wiping away tears. Why? Because his grandson was making a choice. An important one. A life-changing one.

Are you back at your Shechem where you and your house first chose the Lord? It's interesting what Joshua says to the people at Shechem. After he says, "Choose this day whom you will serve," they respond, "Far be it from us that we should forsake the Lord to serve other gods" (Joshua 24:16). After they tell Joshua they'll serve the Lord, Joshua says, No you won't. I quote: "Joshua said to the people, 'You cannot serve the Lord, for he is a holy God. He is a jealous God" (Joshua 24:19).

Do you hear that volley of words?

Joshua: 'Whom will you serve?"

The people: "The Lord."

Joshua: "No you won't."

Huh? That would be like if when I was thirteen-years-old at my Shechem and Reverend Cox asked, "David, do you believe Jesus is the Christ, the Son of living God, and do you accept him as Lord and Savior?" and I said, "I do," he said, "No you don't. You'll forsake the Lord. You'll compromise your convictions. You'll be silent when you need to speak up. You'll go along with the crowd when someone needs to stand up for what is right. You'll withhold your full tithe. You won't forgive others as you've been forgiven. You say you choose God but you won't." Can you imagine?

Or again, I'm imagining my wedding day. The preacher asks, "David, will you have this woman to be your wife to live together in the covenant of marriage? Will you love her, comfort her, honor and keep her in sickness and health, and forsaking all others, will you be faithful to her as long as you both shall live?" I say, "I will." And the pastor that married us said, "No you won't." You say 'I do' today, but your words and deeds won't always match your vows. You say, 'I do' but sometimes you won't."

Can we admit that what Joshua said to the people of Israel and to us is true? When they and we first chose for God, we were all in. Someone asked, "Do you?" And we said, "I do. I do. I do." But 800 years pass and life happens and well, sometimes we don't.

What we need are opportunities to recommit ourselves. To give ourselves again. Joshua took Israel to Shechem and asked them to choose again for the one they chose those many years ago, saying, "Choose this day whom you will serve."

You'll never hear me disparage the annual stewardship campaign because I need opportunities to pledge myself anew to God through Christ. Don't tell me a pledge card is just a piece of paper. When given as an expression of my confession of faith, a tangible sign of my choosing whom I will serve with the fruits of my labor, a handwritten, heartfelt pledge of my desire to be the generous child of our extravagantly giving God, that pledge card is precious in God's sight.

I don't know about you, but I need and I welcome the opportunity to choose again for God. In the first hours of the first day of every week, I need to get up and out of bed and to this sanctuary so that I can choose again to worship the Name above all names. I need that.

In the first hours of every day, I need to be able to choose to set aside my first waking minutes to pray and read a word from scripture, thereby choosing to live that day, God help me, as a disciple of Jesus. I need that.

When it comes right down to it, the annual stewardship campaign is all about holy choices. How will we spend our lives? Whom will we serve? Joshua gathers all the tribes of our congregation to Shechem and he says, "Choose this day whom you will serve."

And we say, "Far be it from us that we should forsake the Lord to serve other gods." We'll serve the Lord!

And Joshua, having heard such promises before says, "You say you will, huh? Well then how about if next Sunday we all gather right here on the brow of Shechem? We'll worship and sing and pray and break the bread and drink the cup and bring our pledges — the firstfruits of our income — and present them to the Lord as a sign of our giving ourselves again. And then to seal it all, we'll have a meal together in the fellowship hall.

And all the clans of Central Christian think to themselves, "Worship, free food, and an opportunity to pledge ourselves anew to God through our tithes and offerings?" And all the clans of Central say, AMEN.

Where Treasure, There Heart

Matthew 6:19-21

Oh, I can just hear those disciples groan. Jesus is talking about money again. "Do not store up for yourselves treasures on earth, where moth and rust consume and where thieves break in and steal" (Matthew 6:19).

Don't you know those disciples are rolling their eyes? They're saying, "There he goes again. Another one of his talks about money. I don't know about you, but I wish he'd just stick to preaching and healing and talking about heaven and leave our pocketbooks alone!"

But that's something Jesus just won't do. Truth be told, money and what we do with it was a favorite topic of our Lord's. Did you know that of Jesus' 43 parables, 27 have to do with money and possessions? Or that one-tenth of the verses in Matthew, Mark, Luke, and John, a tithe of the gospels (288 verses), deal with money? If you thumb through the scriptures you'll find 500 verses on prayer, less than 500 on the topic of faith, but more than 2,000 verses on money.[14]

This is all to say that disciples then and now might wish that Jesus would stay out of pocketbooks and stick to heaven, but our Lord often mentions pocketbook and heaven in the same breath as if maybe, just maybe, there is a relationship between the two. This morning's scripture is a case in point. Jesus said smack dab in the middle of The Sermon on the Mount, "Where your treasure is, there your heart will be also" (Matthew 6:21). Hear that? Treasure and heart. Pocketbook and the heart's desire — heaven. As if they are connected. The Reverend Doctor Dick Hamm, former General Minister and President of the Christian Church (Disciples of Christ), translated Jesus' words, "Wherever you invest your treasure, your heart will surely follow." Or, "If your money's in it, your heart will be, too." The equation is this:

Where treasure, there heart. It's a spiritual truth: if you discover where a person's treasure is, you can be assured that their heart is close by.

Take my two grandfathers, for instance. When I was growing up, I remember spending a lot of time at the home of my maternal grandparents. Looking back to those days, I remember certain things about my grandfather. First thing in the morning, Poppy would go out to get the paper, come back in, sit back in his chair, and immediately turn to a section with a whole bunch of itty bitty letters and numbers all lined up together in columns. Later in the day, when we were out driving in his car, all conversation would stop around noon when Poppy reached out to turn up the volume on the radio in time to hear a radio announcer say something like, "Today's mid-day stock reports are brought to you by...." And later in the day, I recall Poppy going into the den, turning on the television shortly after 6:00 pm, and listening attentively as Doug Adair, the Cleveland TV announcer, talked about "Today's Dow Jones averages." I remember all of that and I remember boring magazines with titles like Forbes and Money that had no pictures whatsoever sitting by Poppy's chair.

What I observed as a child was that my grandfather's mood seemed to swing on what he read in the paper, heard on the radio, watched on television or gleaned from the pages of the boring magazines with no pictures. Some days he was up. Some days he was down. Jesus explained it this way: Where treasure, there heart.

My other grandfather was different. Gabe Shirey was a rounder. When I was little, he used to take me to watch horses run around a big dirt track. Now, I liked horses. I enjoyed looking at all of them. But I couldn't help but to notice that Grandpa seemed to like some horses more than the others — a lot more. In fact, he was real happy for them and liked them a lot when they ran faster than the other horses and he was real sorry for them — even got angry with them — when they didn't run as fast.

My two grandfathers' treasures and hearts were in two very different places, but for both of them, as went their treasure, so went their hearts.

The problem with earthly treasures, says Jesus, is that none of them last. You can't count on them. Whether it's stocks or horses, there's simply no such thing as a "sure thing" when it comes to earthly treasure. Jesus put it this way, "Store up for yourselves treasures in heaven, where neither moth nor rust consumes and where thieves do not break in and steal" (Matthew 6:20).

I found out early the truth of Jesus' words. When I was growing up, I could care less about Poppy's little letters and numbers or Grandpa's horses. My treasure and heart were elsewhere. Namely, in a shoebox in my closet. I want you to know that I caught my little brother once — he was about four or five years old — in my closet. He had opened the shoebox where I kept the baseball cards that I had bought with my hard-earned money from my newspaper route and he had folded my Willie Mays right down the middle. At that moment, I saw no reason to go on living! You see, if you mess with someone's treasure, you mess with their heart. My treasure folded, my heart was broken.

So, where is your treasure? On Wall Street? On hangers in the closet? On four wheels in the driveway? Is your treasure invested in a hobby? In your business? In the roof over your head, the furnishings in your house, the art on the walls, or the lawn wrapped around it all? Is your treasure salted away for retirement or set aside for your children's education or stashed in a shoebox in the closet? Where is your treasure? How much of it is treasure in heaven?

I pondered that question myself this week. Jennie and I were doing some "treasure giving" in the days leading up to April 15, so we had our budget information from the past calendar year readily available. A budget is as good a place as any to look and see where your treasure is. What we did was to chart out the monthly allocations of our treasure last year and what we found was that God came in, well, in the top ten. Fourth to be honest. Behind the taxes we paid to Uncle Sam, the mortgage for the roof over our head, and the food for our bellies came God. It's a humbling exercise, to say the least, to see that in terms of the way David and Jennie Shirey's treasure is invested, God has a firm hold on fourth place. God was just ahead of insurance, clothing, leisure, and furniture. In other words, the Shirey family budget, "the tale of the treasure" if you will, reveals that we have put Uncle Sam first, ourselves second, ourselves third, God fourth, and ourselves in fifth, sixth, seventh, eighth, ninth, and tenth place. What does it say that though we Shireys claim Jesus Christ is our Lord — we say he's first in our hearts — he's fourth in our budget.

Speaking of our budgets, there is nothing wrong with using our earthly treasure to provide for earthly needs and responsibilities. We all have needs for food, clothing, and shelter. Meeting those needs requires a certain amount of earthly treasure. Make no mistake about it, God wants all God's children to have adequate food, shelter, and clothing. That's why the Lord's Prayer invites us to ask God to "give us this day our daily bread." On top of that, we're citizens of a city, state, and nation that make us responsible for the paying of taxes. God expects us to be responsible citizens. Sorry, there are no Bible verses excusing you from paying your taxes. And we must add in our responsibility toward our families. Paul said, "Whoever does not provide for relatives, and especially for family members, has denied the faith and is worse than an unbeliever" (1 Timothy 5:8). Which is all to say that God expects us to lay aside a portion of our earthly treasure to meet our personal needs as well as to meet our responsibilities to family and nation. Our family's budget and I trust yours, too, reflects this.

But here's where being a child of God and follower of Jesus Christ makes a difference (or is supposed to, anyway). In addition to laying up treasure for ourselves, our family, and our nation, he wants us to provide ourselves with treasure in heaven. How so? By creating a budget for blessing, designating a goodly (or godly) portion of our earthly treasure to do heaven's work.

How much is a goodly or godly portion? Throughout our marriage, Jennie and I have set aside a tithe (one-tenth) of our gross income to God's purposes, the greatest portion of that 10% given to the church, the remainder of which we direct to individuals and organizations whose work blesses others. In recent years, we've moved beyond 10% so as to consecrate even more to the glory of God and the blessing of others.

Of course, such giving has left us homeless and chronically hungry. We wear ragged hand-me-downs and have subjected our children to lives of abject poverty. Not! I'm kidding. Sure, we've had times when we wondered if we could really afford to give God a tenth when we were faced with all the personal needs that cried out for our treasure. In those moments, the question arises, "Will I have enough?" If I write that check to the church, will I have enough for next week? For next month? For my kids' education? For their back-to-school clothes? For the car payment? If I give that much to God, will I have enough left for myself? Are you familiar with the question — will I have enough? If you are, as I am, hear Jesus' answer:

"Do not worry about your life, what you will eat or what you will drink, or about your body, what you will wear. Is not life more than food and the body more than clothing? Look at the birds of the air: they neither sow nor reap nor gather into barns, and yet your heavenly Father feeds them. Are you not of more value than they?" (Matthew 6:25, 26).

In response to the age-old question that haunts us, "Will I have enough?," Jesus offers this blessed assurance, "Do not be afraid, little flock, for it is your Father's good pleasure to give you the kingdom" (Luke 12:32).

Now is that just church talk or is it really true? If we create and live by a budget of blessing, putting a tithe of our treasure where our hearts are — invested in God's purposes in this world — will there be enough? If we put God's kingdom first, will everything else follow?

I can only offer my own testimony to the affirmative. When I first heard about tithing years ago, did the math and saw what it amounted to, I thought to myself, "10%!" But someone said to me, "Yep, God gives you everything and lets you keep 90%. What a deal, huh?" Indeed it is. So it is that Jennie and I have budgeted for blessing all along. We've always had enough. And I've passed on to all my congregations the invitation to put our treasure where our hearts are, beginning with Christ's church.

A few years ago, as Jennie and I were planting a new church out in Arizona, meeting in people's homes and then in an elementary school cafeteria, somehow keeping afloat and in ministry one week at a time, we received a check in the mail from a member of one of our first congregations. It was attached to a note that read:

> *Dear David,*
>
> *Sounds like the new church has had quite a year and we hope this check will help support your efforts.*
>
> *In a somewhat related matter, I just want you to know that your influence while at First Christian in Wilmington helped me to realize the true spirit of giving (especially to the church) and it has served me very well throughout the years. By returning my first check of the month to the Lord somehow I've always had enough to meet other needs and still contribute to other missions like your new church start.*
>
> *Hang in there and know Katie and I think of all of you often.*

Part of Mike's heart arrived with his treasure. That's how it works according to our Lord.

I tell you, I have pondered the Lord's words a lot lately. Where treasure, there heart. If that promise is true, then given the way our treasure has been invested since we arrived here and shall continue to be invested, my heart and the hearts of my family are becoming more and more tied to this beloved congregation of which we are a part. A significant portion of our treasure and a significant part of our hearts are right here.

I wouldn't have it any other way. You see, I've decided that Christ's church is a far better home for my treasure and heart than Wall Street, the racetrack, or a shoebox in the closet. Would that one day our full treasure and full hearts be found in the Lord!

Pass The Plates

Deuteronomy 14:22-29

We were in the book of Deuteronomy. One of our daughters thought it was a funny word. The first time she heard it, she repeated it. Said it out loud. Laughed. Then she sang Deuteronomy. Doot-Doot-Eronomy. And I haven't forgotten all these years later. It's a funny word, indeed. From the Greek Deutero nomos. Deutero as in the word deuce — a two. Second. Nomos is the word for law. Second Law. It's Moses repeating God's Law - God's instructions for the fine art of living — a second time. What he said the first time in Exodus he says a second time in Deuteronomy. Isn't that just like us? Needing to be told something twice because we weren't paying attention the first time.

In this case, Moses teaches the people of God about offerings for the second time. I'm guessing he had to say it a second time because they didn't want to listen to him when he talked about money the first time. It doesn't say whether they listened the second time or not. Neither does it say whether you'll listen to me this morning as I explicate what Moses said about making an offering to God. But next Sunday we're all invited to make an offering — namely, an estimate of giving that will undergird our congregation's ministries and mission in the new year. So, let's hear what Moses has to say.

Moses spoke to us about a practice that went back four thousand years. Namely, the tithe. Moses, on God's behalf, said, "Set apart a tithe of all the yield of your seed that is brought in yearly from the field" (Deuteronomy 14:22). Tithe literally means tenth. As in set apart 1/10th of your harvest and bring it to the Lord's House as your offering. You do the math: 1/10th of your paycheck, pension check, social security check, income from investments, tips, commissions, capital gains, dividends.... Did I leave anything out? Now, I don't know what that number feels like to you as you hear Moses' invitation to make an offering to God in gratitude for God's goodness and in support of God's work in this world, but if you ask me, 1/10th — 10% — is getting off easy. I mean, if you left a tenth of your bill at the table as a tip for your server he or she would feel stiffed and wonder, "What did I do wrong to receive only 10 %?" The IRS's lowest tax bracket is 10%. That means if you make more than $10,000 or so a year and send in a tithe to Uncle Sam, you can expect a not-so-cordial letter from the IRS and a stiff penalty. What does it say about God that servers expect 15-20% and Uncle Sam expects somewhere in the neighborhood of 12%, 22%, 24% or more, but the creator of heaven and earth asks for but a tithe? A tenth. It says to me God is gracious and invites us to be gracious and generous in return. Moses said, "Set apart a tithe."

Why? Why the tithe? Moses says, "So that ... you may learn to fear the Lord your God always" (Deuteronomy14:23). Fear means to revere. To honor. Bottom line: when we tithe, give to God first, we're revering and honoring God by giving God first place in our lives, including our budgets. Tithing is simply putting our money where our mouth is. If we say God is first, then we give to God first. A bumper sticker I spotted years ago read, *If you love Jesus, tithe. Any fool can honk.* The question is, do we give God "firstfruits" or leftovers? Is God our first thought or an afterthought? When we tithe, we put our money where our mouth is. We revere God by putting God first and giving God the first tenth.

But get this: What does God choose to do with our tithe? Does God pocket it? *Thank you very much. Ka-ching!* Does God salt it away in some heavenly safe? No. What does God do? God pays our tithes forward to others. Specifically, the Levites (we'll come back to them), the resident aliens, the orphans, and the widows. Here are Moses' words: "You shall bring out the full tithe of your produce... and store it within your towns; the Levites... as well as the resident aliens, the orphans, and the widows in your towns, may come and eat their fill ...

so that the Lord your God may bless you in all the work that you undertake" (Deuteronomy 14:28, 29). That's our God! God wants the tithe not for selfish ends but for God's selfless purposes, beginning with caring for the poor and vulnerable. We're to designate a portion of our cumulative offerings for deeds of mercy and justice for such as the orphan, the widow, and the alien. So it is that when we reach our goal of increasing our giving for next year by 5% we want to increase our outreach giving. Our tithes revere God when we revere God's mandate to love our neighbors in need as we love ourselves. Elsewhere in Deuteronomy, Moses says, "If there is among you anyone in need... do not be hard-hearted or tight-fisted toward your needy neighbor. You should rather open your hand... to meet the need" (Deuteronomy 15:7, 8). Since that directive is part of what is called The Law (the Hebrew word is *Torah*), it dawned on me that since God makes care for others a top line item in God's Law, poverty is literally out-*lawed* in the Old Testament. Chew on that a while. What does God choose to do with our tithes? Pay them forward to care for the aliens (immigrants), orphans, and widows. Not to do so is against *the* law.

But there's more. According to Moses, the Levites are also to receive a portion of the tithe. Who were the Levites? Well, the ministers and staff of the temple. I resemble that remark. As does Elizabeth. And Michael. And Lynn, Mollie, Cindy, Kelly, Carl, and Kim. Bottom line: God directs part of the people's tithes to care for those who care for them. The Levites. In our day and age, I think it's fair to say that includes pastors, preachers, Christian educators, music directors, custodians of the Temple, and administrators of the church. I'll never forget a little father and son talk years ago. I was talking to my son about his giving to the church (or lack thereof). To which he said, "Dad, I'd just be paying your salary." To which I said, "A portion of your offering would, but I hope you think my ministry makes a positive difference in the lives of the people of this congregation and through them in the lives of others near and far. I hope you think my work is worth supporting." And he shrugged and said, "You're my dad." If I was a policeman or a firefighter or a teacher or a veteran, would he demur from paying his taxes because he would be paying his dad's salary? Men and women ordained in the Presbyterian tradition are asked, "Will you pray for and seek to serve the people with energy, intelligence, imagination, and love?"

I hope you know your Levites in this church, though not Presbyterian, strive with all our hearts to do just that. To be a pastor to God's people, a caretaker of the house of the Lord, a teacher of the faith, a director of holy harmonies, an organist or office administrator is a high calling deserving of the greatest effort and highest accountability. According to Moses, those callings are also deserving of the support made possible by a portion of the congregation's offerings.

God directs the people's tithes to care for the alien, widow and orphan, to care for the caregivers, the Levites, and I've saved the best for last. A portion of the tithe is to be used for, well, I don't know how else to say this: a party. Moses says: "Eat the tithe of your grain, your wine, and your oil, as well as the firstlings of your herd and flock... Spend the money for whatever you wish: oxen, sheep, wine, strong drink, or whatever you desire. And you shall eat there in the presence of the Lord your God, you and your household rejoicing together" (Deuteronomy 14:22-26). That sounds to me like the mother of all barbeques. Picnic on the grounds paid for by the tithes!

What I hear in that is that God desires for the offerings of God's people to be used in ways that will promote joyous fellowship. Esprit de corps. Joie de vivre. Church ought to be life giving and joy enhancing. I know some folks have a hard time getting their minds around the thought of words like God, Christians, wine, and celebration in the same sentence. Like the story that's told of a stern-faced teetotaler lady who was asked, "Don't you know Jesus turned water into wine at Cana and served wine to his disciples at the Last Supper?" "Yes," she said, "and I've never forgiven him for it!" Well get over it because the Bible I read tells me the Savior I confess did *what* for his very first sign? He turned water into wine — and lots of the good stuff, no less! That's a sign for me that our Lord delights in our enjoying life together. If your image of God is a stern-faced spoilsport whose only vocabulary words are *No!* and *Shhh!* you're confusing the king of heaven with your seventh grade study hall teacher. God delights in a *good* party. I'm not talking about debauchery. I'm talking about a communal celebration. I'm talking about what the psalmist means when he says, "O taste and see that the Lord is good" (Psalm 34:8). I'm talking about what we used to sing at summer church camp and I've grown to experience firsthand: "I've got that joy, joy, joy, joy down in my heart." I'm talking about the banter that I love in the kitchen among the cooks preparing the monthly Men's Breakfast. I'm talking about the laughter I regularly hear in our office during the week. I'm talking about carrying on in Christ as a holy sacrament. I see faces of Christians sometimes (and during worship no less!) that make me want to pass a bottle of Maalox down the pew. What's up with that? Hear me when I say God rejoices in our rejoicing! So it is that a portion of the tithe is to undergird a community who enjoys making the journey of faith together. Save me from sour-faced, shriveled-soul Christians and direct my tithe, please, to underwriting ministries that enrich, delight, and bring joy in the Lord.

We're in the book of Deuteronomy. *Doot- Doot- Eronomy.* Second Law. Moses had to say it a second time because the people didn't pay attention or didn't want to hear it the first time. But why did he need to invite a tithe a second time? Who, confessing Christ is Lord with their lips, would not also confess with their budget and their giving that God is first? Who wouldn't be glad to give in a way that loves the neighbor and supports the caregivers? Why would I need to be asked a second time to give to something that funds joy and goodness and delight?

Moses says, "Set apart a tithe of all the yield of your seed." Bring your offering to God's House next Sunday and put them in the plates. After worship, at Moses' directive, dinner will be served in Fellowship Hall. Count Jennie and me in. How about you?

Let all God's people say AMEN.

All God's Chil'ren Got Talent

Matthew 25:14-30

Last words. We lean in and listen when someone speaks their last words. The parable of the talents is among Jesus' last words. The parable is in chapter 25 of Matthew's gospel. Chapter 26 is Holy Week. Chapter 27 is the cross. Among the last words of Jesus' public ministry is the Parable of the Talents. What do you need to hear this morning?

For instance, do you need to hear everyone received a talent? That would include you. Are you familiar with the late folk musician Bill Staines' wonderful ditty titled "A Place in the Choir?"

All God's critters got a place in the choir,
Some sing low, some sing higher,
Some sing out loud on a telephone wire,
Some just clap their hands, or paws, or anything they've got.[15]

Well, all God's chil'ren got a place in the choir, too. All God's chil'ren got talent! Every one of us.

While we use the word talent to refer to one's abilities, a talent in Jesus' day was a unit of weight of precious metal equivalent to about 75 pounds worth about $675,000 in today's money. Two talents is over 1.3 million. Five is a whopping 3.4 million. My goodness! According to the parable, God has gifted every single one of us — you included — with a six-figure talent or more. Try not to be conspicuous, but glance at the folks sitting next to you, in front of you, and behind you. What does it feel like to be sitting among folks carrying anywhere from 675 grand to 3.4 million? The parable says everyone has a talent.

I mention this biblical promise because some people have convinced themselves they have no talent. Believing such a lie has two devastating consequences — it diminishes the self-esteem of the individual and it diminishes the ministry of Christ's church. I ache for people who have convinced themselves (or have allowed others to convince them) they have no talent, that they have nothing to offer. Somebody said, "Everybody is a ten somewhere" and I've always believed that. To the point that when I welcome a new member, I can't help but wonder what God-given gifts they bring into the fellowship of the church. Everyone has been given a talent — 75 pounds of gold-plated, God-given precious metal talent. Therefore, everyone is to be accorded the dignity incumbent upon such divinely gifted people.

Or do you need to hear that one of the recipients of God-given talent buried his talent? In the parable, the donor of the talents attributed that to laziness. "You wicked and lazy slave!" (Matthew 25:26), he said. But as I was pondering this passage, I thought of all the reasons I've observed in my years of ministry as to why some people bury their talents; reasons that evoke not judgment but understanding and sympathy.

For instance, I've known people who buried their talent because someone criticized them at some point for their use of their talent. People can say some thoughtless, insensitive things, but few are more devastating than when we criticize someone's sincere effort at using their talent. Some people have been hurt so deeply by callous criticism that they determine to bury their talent so deeply they'll never be vulnerable to criticism again.

Other people have buried their talent because though having once joyfully stepped up and offered it, they were never allowed a season of rest from using their gift and got burned out. It doesn't matter if your gift is teaching, singing, greeting, decorating, preparing coffee, or preparing communion, some people offered their gifts only to feel after years of serving in the same role that they had received a life sentence without parole. So, when given half a chance, they ducked out, buried their gift, and never offered it again.

Some bury their gift because they were never thanked for

using it. "Since no one seemed to appreciate my gift when I offered it, maybe they won't notice it when it's buried ten feet under and I'm not doing it anymore."

Others bury their gift because they compare their gift with others and dismiss their talent as inferior or insignificant.

Still others bury their gift because they can't imagine it has any value. They can't see how what they enjoy doing might contribute to the growth of the church or its upbuilding in love. Or no one ever asked them what their gift was, let alone invited them to share it. So, they buried it. "I didn't mention it because no one asked, and I didn't think it mattered."

Some people didn't bury their talent as much as the church forced them to keep it hidden in a closet under wraps, unwelcome and unwanted.

- I'm speaking of women in explicitly patriarchal churches who hear there is no place for your talent if you were born without a Y chromosome.
- I'm speaking of youth who may hear, "You're the church of tomorrow, but not today."
- I am speaking of those who are new to a congregation and get the strong impression they need to wait until they've been there a few decades before they can participate. Wait a few more decades after that and maybe they can be a leader.
- And you know as well as I do that a lot of people have been told to keep their God-given, precious talent buried or closeted.

I give thanks ours is a church where all people who desire to offer their talents are welcome to do so and where those who have long-buried gifts can find the healing and affirmation that invites the unearthing of long-buried gifts so they may be offered anew.

I hasten to add this: the reason the one talent recipient gave for burying his talent was that he was afraid of the master. "Master," he said, "I knew that you were a harsh man, reaping where you did not sow, and gathering where you did not scatter seed; so I was afraid, and I went and hid your talent in the ground" (Matthew 25:25).

Do you need to hear this morning that the master in the parable who is arrogant, greedy, ruthless, and fearful — is not God? I ask that because some of us have been taught (or just assumed) that a parable is a simple allegory with a one-to-one correspondence and to figure it out you just equate the authority figure in the parable with God and the other people in it with us. In which case, this parable would mean we're the receivers of talent. God is the master. And we'd better double what we've been given or else wailing and gnashing of teeth for you. I mention this because some people are raised to be afraid of God and if you live life afraid of God, you'll serve God just to avoid punishment and live life with a knot in your stomach and a burgeoning resentment in your soul. Nobody likes to be bullied and nobody loves a bully.

No life can fully flourish and flower if it's planted in the soil of fear. Which is why I said that maybe you need to hear that this master, a harsh man, a man who stirred paralyzing fear in the man with the one talent, is not the God who was made known to us by Jesus Christ. To the contrary, our God "so loved the world that he gave his only Son… God did not send the Son into the world to condemn the world, but in order that the world might be saved through him" (John 3:16, 17). If you've ever been on the receiving end of fearmongering religion where every Sunday the smell of burning sulfur is in the air, maybe you needed to hear that fear-inducing god is a small-g imposter god. You were created, redeemed and accorded a six-figure talent by loving capital-G God who poured himself out even unto death on a cross. God is love: "Love divine, all loves excelling... Pure, unbounded love thou art."16

Maybe that's something we all need to hear this morning: that God is love. Because when you know that God is not a fearful ogre but rather a loving source and force for goodness and grace, you'll live your life out of gratitude and generosity.

As the great hymn puts it, "Were the whole realm of nature mine, that were a present far too small. Love so amazing, so divine, demands my soul, my life, my all."17

You see, theology matters. What you believe is what you'll become. Fear begets fear. Unrelenting judgment begets unrelenting judgment. Festering anger begets festering anger. But love evokes love. Generosity evokes generosity. Giving evokes giving. Affirmation evokes affirmation. Welcome evokes welcome. Maybe we all needed to hear this morning that we don't need to be afraid of God but rather we can revere God whose giving knows no ending. "The Lord, the Lord, a God merciful and gracious, slow to anger, and abounding in steadfast love and faithfulness" (Exodus 34:6).

I'll be honest with you. I'll tell you what I was afraid of when I first came here. I was afraid this church, being an historic downtown church, might be staid, stuffy, and stuck-up, a museum of religious relics, and as such, that you were looking for some crusty curator to come and conserve and preserve everything in your 200-year-old collection. I was afraid to accept the call to come here because it's the inclination of some historic cathedral churches to sit on their inheritance, bury their talents, and form a holy clique impermeable to anyone on the outside who may try to get in. I didn't want any part of that. I was afraid.

I'm so glad I can say this morning that my fears were misplaced. This is no musty museum. This is a spirit-filled mission station whose windows are wide open to the mystery and majesty of the winds of the Spirit. I'm so glad the focus of Central is not backward but forward. What Pope John XXIII said years ago about the mission of the church is true. Namely, "We're not on earth to guard a museum, but to cultivate a flourishing garden of life." This congregation is entering a third century of ministry and mission with talents galore and is growing each week with new members gladly stepping to the altar with their gifts. This is a congregation that extends its welcome to one and all in a manner that says, "No matter who you are, take out your talent. Dig it up, if need be. Don't be afraid. Shake off the dust and dirt and share your talent to the glory of God and the service of others near and far.

Jennie and I will put our pledge in the offering plate — a full tithe, 10% of our talent — this morning without reservation. Without fear. With gladness and gratitude. Join us, good and faithful servants, and "enter into the joy of your master" (Matthew 25:21).

A Great Commandment Congregation

Mark 12:28-34

It's called The Great Commandment: "You shall love the Lord your God with all your heart, and with all your soul, and with all your mind, and with all your strength" and "You shall love your neighbor as yourself." (Mark 12:30, 31) Jesus' contemporaries in the first century had identified 613 individual commandments in Scripture. 248 "Thou shalts" and 365 "Thou shalt nots." One of the scribes asked, "Which commandment is the first of all?" (Mark 12:28)

What's your gut reaction to the word commandment? When you hear the word commandment do you hear "Obey them or else" accompanied by the image of some red-faced preacher spanking a black leather Bible and shaking a boney finger who has been deputized by a God who's out to get you? I hope not. The commandments in the Bible are not for guilt trips but good trips. As in good trips through life. As in Jesus saying of God's commandments: "Do this and you will live" (Luke 10:28). Jesus came that we "may have life and have it abundantly" (John 10:10). Commandments are given by our good and gracious God not to guilt us but to good us, bless us by pointing the way to a good life — the good life.

Jesus didn't say of the Great Commandment, "Memorize this commandment" or "Think about this commandment" or "Talk about this commandment." He says, "Do this, and you will live" (Luke 10:28). If doing the commandments spell life, then doing the Great Commandment promises a great life. Not great as in fame and fortune, but great as in fulfillment and satisfaction. Great as in living life "not far from the kingdom" (Mark 12:34). If that's the case, bring it on!

Which raises the question: how would we go about doing the Great Commandment? I think the answer lies in the phrase "first of all" as in "Which commandment is the first of all?"

I used to hear "Which commandment is the first of all" as meaning "In the Bible's top ten list of commandments, what's #1?" But this week I heard the phrase "first of all" as "First of all, do this." The word translated "first" is protos in Greek. Proto as in original. As in prototype. As in priority. I hear Jesus saying, "Give priority to loving God and neighbor. Do this first and you will live."

I asked myself, What are some concrete ways I can love God first of all— make that a priority in my life? And I remembered somebody saying once there are two things that show what our priorities are — our calendars and our checkbook. So, how can we put love of God first of all in those two things?

As for putting God first of all in our calendars, we're doing that right now. Think about it: it's the first day of the week and here we are first thing in the morning and with our first waking hours we're giving our hearts, souls, minds, and might to loving God. That's what worship's all about, right? As for loving God with all our minds, we spend the first hours of the first day opening the Bible so as to dig into it, pore over it, and reflect on it. And to the degree that Monday through Saturday we first of all spend the first fifteen minutes of the day in prayer or meditation or reading Scripture or journaling, we're making the love of God a priority on our calendars. Not to mention at mealtimes first of all pausing to give thanks. Or before making any decision, first of all considering how my faith can inform what I do. These are all concrete and specific ways of putting God first of all on our calendars.

What would it mean to put God first of all in the checkbook? Well, we're invited to do that today. This is Thanksgiving Sunday of our annual stewardship campaign. We're invited to place our estimates of giving for the coming year in the offering plates, which can't be done unless we consider our personal budgets and ask, "First of all, what will I give to God through the ministries of the church?" I know that if I don't intentionally put God first in my giving each week or each month, God will get not my firstfruits, but leftovers.

Brian Kluth used a nifty illustration to make that same point.18 He said if you've ever had a vest or a button down sweater, you know how important it is to get the first button fastened correctly. When the first button is in the wrong place, every other one will be out of order — and you'll end up with a mess. The same is true with stewardship of our finances. If we don't fasten our giving button first, first of all make our offering to God, all our other financial buttons (saving, spending, investing) will be out of order, and we'll end up with a problem needing to be rectified." So, before a new year begins, I first estimate my gift to God.

When we love God concretely and specifically in our calendars and checkbooks, we're doing the commandment to love God with heart, soul, mind, and might with our time and treasure.

But there's more to the Great Commandment. Jesus adds, "And love your neighbor as yourself" (Mark 12:31). In other words, what do you want for yourself and your loved ones? Want all those things for others, too, and take action to make them possible for others. That's love of neighbor.

I remember learning Abraham Maslow's Hierarchy of Needs way back when. He drew a pyramid with what he called "Basic Needs" at the bottom: food, water, warmth, and rest. Safety and security. Do you want those? Everybody does. Love others by working to see that everyone has food, water, warmth, and shelter and everybody's neighborhood is safe and secure. Up the pyramid Maslow had what he called: "Belongingness and Esteem needs." Do you want respect, dignity, and love? Certainly you do. Love your neighbor as yourself by advocating that everybody everywhere is accorded the same. At the top of the pyramid Maslow places what he calls "Self-actualization" — being able to fulfill your potential. Do you want an education, opportunities to create and contribute and earn and advance? Go for it, and at the same time make sure everybody else can, too. Love your neighbor is not spelled l-u-v and accomplished by blowing a kiss. It's accomplished by acts of mercy and justice that provide and advocate for everyone else to have the truly good things in life you want for yourself and your loved ones.

The Great Commandment: "Love God with heart, soul, and mind. Love your neighbor as yourself." The Great Commandment is not just for individual Christians to aspire to; it's also for churches. Though every congregation may have a ministry and mission uniquely tailored to its context that is dependent on its location, its people's gifts and graces, and its surrounding community's needs, surely all churches are called to be first and foremost Great Commandment congregations, their ministries focused on loving God and loving neighbors.

Think of five of our congregation's foundational ministries:

1. Our centuries-long commitment to education for discipleship.
2. Our passion for worship "in spirit and in truth" (John 4:24) in a sanctuary that embraces us in "the beauty of holiness" (Psalm 96:9 KJV).
   Those two add up to "Love God with heart, soul, mind, and strength."
3. Our longstanding provision of welcome and hospitality to one and all.
4. Our willingness to grapple with the vexing social and moral issues of the day.
5. Our commitment to outreach through ministries of mercy and justice.

Those three add up to "Love your neighbor as yourself." Every congregation's ministries will be variations on that theme. All churches are called to be Great Commandment congregations.

I asked myself as Jennie and I filled out our estimate of giving card for the coming year, "What kind of legacy do I want to contribute to?" And it dawned on me — I want to give of my time, talent and treasure to a place and people who "first of all" are about the business of loving God and loving neighbor, people who do the Great Commandment.

A man by the name of Sheldon Van Aucken wrote a book entitled "Severe Mercy." It was a compilation of letters he had written to C.S. Lewis when he was searching for God but had not yet made a Christian commitment. In one of the letters, he wrote, "The strongest argument I have yet for Christianity is Christians. Their love, most of all. Their joy, as well. Their certainty of things to come. The strongest argument I have found yet against Christianity is also Christians. When they are somber and joyless, when they are self-righteous and complacent. When they are narrow, judgmental, and repressive, lacking love, then Christianity dies a thousand deaths in my mind."19

I want to be part of a congregation that is a compelling argument in favor of Christianity. I want to be part of a Great Commandment congregation.

Mark tells us that when the scribe heard Jesus' answer as to which commandment is first of all, he said, "You are right, Teacher" (Mark 12:32). Darn right, Jesus is right! There's nothing like living life doing the Great Commandment heart, soul, mind, and might, living it out with calendar and checkbook, loving God and neighbor with our time, talent, and treasure.

When Jesus saw that he answered wisely, he said to him, "You are not far from the kingdom of God" (Mark 12:34). So true! When we're living life day by day with love of God and neighbor "first of all" in all we do, it's a sweet place to be. We're not far from the kingdom.

As we prepare to make the offering of our living and giving, let all God's people say AMEN.

The Master's Math

John 6:1-14

The feeding of the 5,000. Aside from the resurrection, it's the only miracle recorded in all four Gospels. Matthew, Mark, Luke, and John must have thought it's an important story. It is.

The first thing to note is this: miracles begin when someone notices a need. Emphasis on the word notice. My good friend Johnny Wray, retired executive director of Week of Compassion, the Christian church (Disciples of Christ)'s worldwide relief and development ministry, says, "Before we can engage in the simplest deeds of mercy and kindness, first we must notice." In our scripture, Jesus noticed "a great crowd coming toward him" (John 6:5). A lot of hungry people. I mention this because it's possible not to notice need. I'll never forget the story one of my colleagues, Jim Crouch, told about a trip he made to India. As he was walking down a crowded street among a sea of beggars, his host whispered, "Just don't look them in the eye." Do you hear what he was saying? Try not to notice. There's a Haitian proverb that says, "What the eye doesn't see, doesn't move the heart." And when the heart isn't moved, the mind isn't moved to consider what might be done and our hands and feet aren't moved to do something. To care, we first have to notice. We have to be willing to look them in the eye as Jesus did who "looked up and saw a great crowd" of hungry people.

The sight of them filled Jesus with compassion. In Mark's telling of the story, he says, "He saw a great crowd; and he had compassion for them, because they were like sheep without a shepherd" (Mark 6:34). They had no food and no clue; were without food and without direction. The word is compassion, one of the treasured vocabulary words in the Bible. "Jesus had compassion." That refrain appears at least twenty times in the gospels. If the gospels were a song, the chorus would be "and

Jesus had compassion." He embraced the weary. He touched the lepers. He cradled Jairus' daughter in his arms. The great hymn of the church sings, "Jesus thou art all compassion, pure unbounded love thou art."20

Look at the word. It's made up of two parts: com (with) + passion (suffer) = to suffer with. I don't expect you to know Greek, the language in which the New Testament was written, so I'll tell you that the Greek word translated compassion is splanknizomai. It's a messy-sounding word, isn't it? You feel like you should wear a bib when you say compassion in its original language to avoid getting some of it on you. No wonder it's such a messy-sounding word. Splanknizomai literally means "to tear your bowels up." When we say something is "gut-wrenching" or something is "tearing us up," we're bearing witness to the root meaning of compassion. I don't know what's tearing you up these days, what human hurt is on your heart, but I want you to know that Jesus notices human suffering and it tears him up. He has compassion.

What does he do? He turns to Philip and asks, "Where are we to buy bread for these people to eat?" (John 6:5). Notice the pronoun Jesus used: we. Where shall we buy bread? Apparently, this is going to be a cooperative undertaking, a joint venture between the Son of God and faithful sons and daughters of God. Reaching out to meet human need isn't a solo effort on Jesus' part: "Where will I buy bread?" This being a miracle story, couldn't Jesus simply have snapped his fingers and provided 5,000 hot meals, forks, spoons, knives, and linen napkins to boot? Voila. That would have been a miracle! But he didn't. Instead, he invited the disciples to be part of the offering. Serving others is a partnership of heaven and earth, the Lord and the Lord's people. Jesus asks, "Where shall we buy bread for these people to eat?"

Philip answered him, "Six months' wages would not buy enough bread for each of them to get a little" (John 6:7). The Revised Shirey Translation reads, "Heck if I know where we're going to find enough bread. We sure don't have enough." Philip is overwhelmed with need and understocked with resources. There are 5,000 of them and twelve of us. It's called the scarcity mindset: the belief that we don't have enough. We focus on the word generosity this time of the year as we consider what we'll offer God in the year ahead, but the capacity for generosity is precluded by a mindset of scarcity. Listen carefully to that word: scare-city. Citizens of Scare City don't have enough for themselves let alone enough to share with anybody else.

It's not just money we don't have enough of. How many times do I hear someone say, "There's just not enough time in the day!" From the beginning of time, there's been the same amount of time — 24 hours in a day. What is it about our lifestyle that convinces us we don't have enough time? If we think we don't have enough time — "Can't you see I'm busy?" — we won't have time to help someone else.

We don't have enough space, either. Studies say the average American home went from 1,660 square feet in 1973 to over 2,500 square feet these days. That's a 50 % increase. But apparently we still don't have enough space because we rent off-site storage spaces to hold all the stuff we spent the money we don't have enough of to buy, enough time to use, or enough space to store!

Philip and so many people live in scare-city: we don't have enough. Generosity, (or shall I pronounce it generos-city) and scare-city are miles apart.

Jesus didn't excuse his disciples from showing compassion by saying, "I know you don't have enough bread. Just forget it. Sorry I asked. I'll take care of this on my own." No, he extended his hands and said, "Give me what you have. Whatever time, whatever talent, whatever energy you have, bring it to me and we'll see what we can do together."

Whereupon Andrew spoke up. "There is a boy here who has five barley loaves and two fish. But what are they among so many people?" (John 6:8-9). Andrew had no idea what difference the boy's little bit might make, but he was willing to give Jesus what he had. He had his doubts, but he also had faith. Good for Andrew! He handed Jesus the loaves and fishes then Jesus took it from there.

Andrew was willing to trust in what Dr. Alyce McKenzie, Professor of Preaching and Worship at Perkins School of Theology, calls the Jesus Factor.

"The disciples' job," she said, "is to factor Jesus into any challenging situation they may face, and to count on his presence and power from now on. They are to be those who call on the Jesus factor in all situations. What is the Jesus factor? The Jesus factor is the fact, emphasized over and over again by John, that Jesus is present and ready to help in any situation of need... The disciples' job is to witness to and share that Jesus factor with others." 21

Trusting in the Jesus factor, Andrew offered what he had to Jesus. And what did Jesus do? "Jesus took the loaves, and when he had given thanks, he distributed them to those who were seated; so also the fish, as much as they wanted" (John 6:11). My goodness! 12 disciples + 5 loaves + 2 fish x 1 Jesus = 5,000 fed. Call it the algebra of the almighty, the calculus of the Christ, the trigonometry of The Trinity, the geometry of generosity. I don't understand the miracle of the master's math, how all that adds up. But because it does, I believe a congregation that is willing to notice need and give whatever we have to Jesus can feed thousands — body, mind, and soul.

What's more, as we do, so we'll be fed ourselves. Jennie taught me tithing four decades ago when we married. All these years we've given God ten percent of our income and on top of that we've been involved in more capital campaigns than you can shake a pledge card at. Yet, somehow our three kids have never missed a meal, a change of clothes, or an education. It's the master's math again: *5 Shireys – 10% x the Jesus factor = Enough.* It's a miracle!

John told us, "Jesus took the loaves, and when he had given thanks, he distributed them to those who were seated; so also the fish, as much as they wanted." (John 6:11). Did you catch those verbs? Jesus took what they offered him, blessed, broke, and gave it. That's communion language. I don't think it's a coincidence that John uses the language of worship to describe the offering that day. Whenever we offer our time, talent, and treasure to God to take, bless, and distribute to others — that is a communion of God and God's people that is worship pure and true.

Every November, Jesus comes to his disciples and asks us, "How are we going to feed thousands of people next year body, mind, and spirit?" We then bring what we have — five loaves, two fish, a tithe — whatever. We give our offerings to Jesus and he takes it from there.

It's happening again. I went home for lunch on Thursday and smelled something. I sniffed, looked around, and saw what it was. It was sitting on the kitchen table. Our pledge card had come in the mail. It smelled like loaves and fishes! Yes, indeed. Our pledges + five loaves + two fish x one Jesus = thousands of bodies, minds, and spirits fed in ministry and mission in the new year.

Let all who trust the master's math say AMEN.

The Indescribable Gift

2 Corinthians 9:6-15

The apostle Paul is known for many things. His dramatic conversion on the Damascus Road for starters. One minute he's Christianity's fiercest foe, the next Christ's most ardent advocate. Or, his letters to the first Christian churches — first postmarked from prison, now posted in the New Testament. He experienced the highest highs — "Caught up to the third heaven — whether in the body or out of the body I do not know" (2 Corinthians 12:2). And he endured the lowest lows — "Three times I have been beaten with rods. Once I received a stoning. Three times I was shipwrecked" (2 Corinthians 11:24, 25).

All of the above witness to Paul's passion for the gospel. But did you know one of Paul's proudest endeavors for the cause of Christ was an offering? 22 That's right. One of the crown jewels of his ministry was an offering he received for the churches in Jerusalem. That offering, and the stewardship campaign that led up to it, gave Paul as much joy and satisfaction as anything.

Paul closes his appeal letter to the congregation in Corinth by writing, "Thanks be to God for his indescribable gift!" (2 Corinthians 9:15). So much for preachers and congregations who dread the annual stewardship campaign. So much for all the jokes about passing the offering plate: "Did you say offering plate? I'll pass." Paul didn't get the memo about being reluctant to invite God's people to respond with gratitude to God's grace. To the contrary, he wrote two chapters, 2 Corinthians 8 and 9, that unabashedly announce an offering, tout "cheerful giving" (2 Corinthians 9:7), and end with downright exuberance: "Thanks be to God for his indescribable gift!" The noun is gift. The adjective is indescribable. The Greek word translated indescribable is found only here in the New Testament.

It's difficult to translate. How do you adequately translate something that means "beyond human description?" Some Bible scholars suggest "ineffable."23 I'll settle for indescribable followed by an exclamation mark.

That raises a question: What is this indescribable gift so rare, so precious, that Paul uses a one-of-a-kind word to describe it?

Some say the indescribable gift may refer to the first-of-its-kind show of Christian unity the offering represents. You see, Paul received the offering from the Gentile Christians of Galatia, Corinth, and Macedonia for the Jewish Christians in Jerusalem. Apparently, the brothers and sisters in Jerusalem were in need. Paul saw Gentiles sending gifts to Jews as a powerful sign that the kingdom of God was at hand. After all, Gentiles and Jews lived in a simmering state of distrust and animosity. To have Gentiles dig deeply into their pockets to send an offering to support Jews — why, that would be like Sunnis sending a caravan of relief trucks to Shiites or Jerusalem Jews writing a check to West Bank Palestinians. No wonder some scholars think Paul viewed Gentile Christians taking up an offering for Jewish Christians as an "indescribable gift."

Other scholars think it refers to the overwhelming generosity Paul saw in the Christians in Macedonia and Corinth. He invited a gift and they responded beyond all imagining. As Paul put it, their giving "overflowed in a wealth of generosity... They voluntarily gave according to their means and even beyond their means" (2 Corinthians 8:2, 3). In a word, their gift was indescribable.

One thing's for sure. That offering evidenced to Paul that their newfound faith was sincere. He wrote: "Through the testing of this ministry you glorify God by your obedience to the confession of the gospel of Christ and by the generosity of your partnership with them and with all others" (2 Corinthians 9:13). Paul refers to the offering as a test of their confession. That is, they confessed with their lips that Christ is Lord. In him, they committed to loving God and neighbor. Now, by the obedience of their generosity, they put their money where their mouths are. The offering was a test of their confession and they passed with flying colors. They gave an indescribable gift.

Paul knew as well as you and I do that talk is cheap. It's one thing to open your mouth and say, "I love God and neighbor." It's another to open your pocketbook. There's a bumper sticker that says, "If you love Jesus, tithe. Any fool can honk." Or, as I heard a preacher say while holding up his offering envelope and looking heavenward, "No matter what I say or do, this is what I think of you." Those Macedonians and Corinthians were willing to practice the gospel they professed. Their indescribable gift was a megaphone of praise and thanksgiving to God.

So, what was the indescribable gift? Was it the unprecedented act of Gentiles taking up an offering for Jews? Was it the outpouring of generosity that came from their giving according to their means and beyond? Was it newly baptized Christians proving the sincerity of their faith by their good confession ushering in a great offering? All of those were indescribable gifts, but they don't add up to the indescribable gift.

The indescribable gift is Jesus. Jesus is the gift from God that motivates all expressions of grace, gratitude, and generosity. Jesus is the gift so precious, so rare, so beyond human description that Paul uses a one-of-a-kind, once-in-the-Bible word to describe him: indescribable. A woman once told me of a friend who became disgusted with the church. She threw up her hands and said, "I've had enough of the politics, the hypocrisy, the pettiness, the judgmentalism, and the inefficiency of how things are done around here. I've had it with the church. Stick a fork in me. I'm done." She became a Unitarian. A few years later, her friend returned. "I bet I know why you're back," the woman said. "You found politics, hypocrisy, pettiness, judgmentalism, and inefficiency in the Unitarian fold, too." To which her friend said, "No, I missed Jesus."

I understand. How 'bout you? I can't imagine my life without God's indescribable gift of Jesus Christ:

- without his people — you!
- without being able to worship and pray and sing in his name.
- without being part of his body, the church, that strives for justice and mercy and truth and beauty and reconciliation, "glorifying God and enjoying God forever."[24]
- without being carried by the winds of his Spirit.
- without his teachings, his example, and his sacrifice.

There may have been a time in my life when I took Jesus for granted, but I don't take him or any of his blessings for granted any more. And every year, when the stewardship campaign rolls around, I see it as an opportunity to give myself again to him.

I remember a story I heard years ago from a colleague, the late Reverend Doctor Bill Nichols. He told of when Victoria was queen of the British Empire. Once, while she was visiting India, she was told that a young prince of a minor province wanted to make a presentation to her.

"Show him in," she said.

The young prince — really just a small child — came in and knelt before the queen. Then he stood, reached into his pocket, and held out a small cloth bag. The queen's attendant opened the bag. A large, brilliant, polished diamond fell into his hand. The queen's attendants gasped, each one whispering to the other about the gigantic size of the stone. Queen Victoria thanked the young prince and promised him that his generous gift would become a permanent part of the royal treasury of crown jewels in London.

Many years later, the young prince made a trip to England. He asked to see the aging queen. She was reminded of the young man's earlier gift and granted him an audience. After the proper introductions were made, the young man asked if he might see the diamond he had given to the queen many years before. It was brought from the vault and handed to him.

"Your Highness," he said, "Years ago when I was a small child, I gave this diamond to you. At that time I had no idea how much this stone was worth. Now I am a man. Now I know how much this is really worth. May I give it to you again, this time with all my heart?"

Dr. Nichols said, "Every time you make a pledge to God through the church, every time you put your tithe in the offering plate, you are reconfirming your confession of faith, renewing the commitment you once made to God. When you make a pledge, you are saying to God, 'Now that I know what life is all about, now that I know what commitment costs, may I give myself to you again?'" 25

Don't ever minimize the significance of the annual stewardship campaign, the making of an offering, the presentation of a pledge. It's the season of the year when we bring the offering of our firstfruits into God's sanctuary and place them on the altar, saying, "Lord God, now that we know how much life in your Son is really worth, we give ourselves again and with our whole hearts."

"Thanks be to God for his indescribable gift!" AMEN.

Endnotes

1. Dean Snyder, "It is about the money: Against docetic offertory prayers," *The Christian Century*, March 1, 2012.
2. I regret I did not keep the bibliographic details on the article. All I kept were my notes on its salient points.

3. Quoted in Adam Hamilton, *Enough: Discovering Joy Through Simplicity and Generosity* (Nashville: Abingdon Press, 2009).

4. Ronald J. Allen, "The Sacramental Tithe" in *Joyful Giving* (St. Louis: Chalice Press, 1997), pp. 67-74.

5. How, William W. "We Give Thee But Thine Own." In the public domain.

6. I am indebted to the late Rev. Al Winn, a Presbyterian pastor whose ministry was formative in my wife's faith formation and whose insights on stewardship influenced me early in my ministry, especially a brochure titled "A Stewardship Tour of the Bible" and a sermon titled "Tithing Is More Than the Number Ten."

https://digital.history.pcusa.org/islandora/object/islandora%3A143224?display=grid#page/1/mode/1up

https://digital.history.pcusa.org/islandora/object/islandora%3A143300#page/1/mode/1up

Also Brian Kluth, "Understanding the Grace of Giving" https://www.kluth.org/people/grace.htm

7. Chisholm, Thomas O. "Great Is Thy Faithfulness." In the public domain.

8. Elizabeth O'Conner. *Letters to Scattered Pilgrims.* (HarperCollins, 1982).

9. Havergall, Frances R. "Take My Life." In the public domain.

10. Watts, Isaac. "When I Survey the Wondrous Cross." In the public domain.

11. Havergal, Frances R. "Take My Life." In the public domain.

12. Anna Carter Florence, "Smashing Beauty," *Journal for Preachers*, Pentecost, 2004).

13. Bob Dylan, "Gotta Serve Somebody," first track on *Slow Train Coming*, Columbia Records, 1979.

14. Herb Miller, *Money Isn't/Is Everything: What Jesus Said About the Spiritual Power of Money* (Discipleship Resources, 1994), p. 3.

15. Bill Staines. "A Place in the Choir." *The Whistle of the Jay*. 1979.

16. Wesley, Charles. "Love Divine, All Loves Excelling." In the public domain.

17. Watts, Isaac. "When I Survey the Wondrous Cross." In the public domain.

18. Brian Kluth, "Understanding the Grace of Giving" https://www.kluth.org/people/grace.htm

19. quoted by Dave Johnson in "Lead With Love," a sermon delivered at Ginghamsburg Church, August 7-8, 1999.

20. Charles Wesley. "Love Divine, All Loves Excelling." In the public domain.

21. In the sermon titled "Mind the Gap: The Feeding of the 5,000." https://www.patheos.com/progressive-christian/mind-the-gap-alyce-mckenzie-07-20-2012

22. It is mentioned in his letters to the Romans (15:25-29), 1 Corinthians (16:1-4), and Galatians (2:10).

23. https://www.biblegateway.com/resources/ivp-nt/Results-Generous-Giving

24. The Presbyterians' Westminster Catechism says "Humanity's chief end is to glorify God, and to enjoy him forever."

25. I heard Dr. Nichols tell this story in person years ago. It appears in print in Dan Moseley, "May I Give Myself Again?" *Joyful Giving* (St. Louis: Chalice Press, 1997), pp. 1- 4.

www.ingramcontent.com/pod-product-compliance
Lightning Source LLC
LaVergne TN
LVHW050937080826
845145LV00004B/1300